*"Whether you are a believer or merely a curious sceptic, this book will help you to discover Jesus as he really is."*

**Sandy Millar – co-founder** of The Alpha Course **and former vica**

*"Original, s*

**R.T. Kendall** ~~Total~~

*Forgiveness*

*"In his distinctively provocative way, Phil Moore presents to us Jesus in full colour. Just like the Jesus it describes, you won't find it boring."*

**Andrew Wilson – Author of *If God, Then What?***

*"What a book! It unleashes the most extraordinary figure in history. After reading it you will love him or hate him, but you will never be the same again."*

**PJ Smyth – GodFirst Church, Johannesburg, South Africa**

*"This short book is downright dangerous! It demands attention. Prepare to be shocked, undone, and put back together again."*

**Greg Haslam – Senior Pastor, Westminster Chapel, London, UK**

# GAGGING JESUS

## THINGS JESUS SAID
## WE WISH HE HADN'T

## Phil Moore

### MONARCH
### BOOKS

Oxford, UK & Grand Rapids, Michigan, USA

Published by Monarch Books
an imprint of
**Lion Hudson plc**
Wilkinson House, Jordan Hill Road,
Oxford OX2 8DR, England
Email: monarch@lionhudson.com
www.lionhudson.com / monarch

ISBN 978 0 85721 453 9
e-ISBN 978 0 85721 454 6

First edition 2013

**Acknowledgments**
Scripture quotations taken from the Holy Bible, New
International Version, copyright © 1973, 1978, 1984, 2011
International Bible Society. Used by permission of Hodder
& Stoughton, a member of the Hodder Headline Group. All
rights reserved. 'NIV' is a trademark of International Bible
Society. UK trademark number 1448790.

A catalogue record for this book is available from the
British Library

Printed and bound in the UK, May 2013, LH26

# Contents

# INTRODUCTION:
# GAGGING JESUS

Jesus of Nazareth wasn't afraid to tell it like it is. Those who claim to follow him, on the other hand, often are.

If we're not careful, we can settle for a tamed and domesticated Jesus, a gagged-and-bound Jesus, a wouldn't-say-boo-to-a-goose Jesus, a Jesus of our own making. But he isn't the real Jesus.

If you have ever suspected that Jesus wasn't crucified for acting like a respectable vicar in a pair of socks and sandals, then this book is for you. It focuses on the fifteen most outrageous aspects of Jesus' teaching – the fifteen things that you are least likely to hear preached in churches today. They are the fifteen things which make most people want to gag him. They are also the things which got him killed.

People have been trying to gag Jesus for 2,000 years. They have tried to sit him on their knee like a ventriloquist's dummy and turn him into a spokesman for their own cause. You can tell how successful they have been from the fact that the gagged-and-bound

Jesus is so popular. He never ruffles feathers because he says exactly what we want to hear.

The Communists tried to gag Jesus. They told the world he was a Communist, just like them. The Soviet president Mikhail Gorbachev argued that *"Jesus was the first socialist, the first to seek a better life for mankind."* The Cuban leader Fidel Castro insisted that *"I never saw a contradiction between the ideas that sustain me and the ideas of that symbol, of that extraordinary figure."*[1]

The enemies of Communism tried to gag Jesus too. Rather suspiciously, they told the world he was a liberal Westerner and a free-thinking capitalist, just like them. The American president John Quincy Adams declared in one of his Fourth of July speeches that *"The birthday of this nation is indissolubly linked with the birthday of the Saviour… It forms a leading event in the progress of the Gospel."*[2] President Richard Nixon cursed and schemed and lied his way through five years in the White House, but that didn't stop him from invoking Jesus as an ally in his speeches and from ending them with a confident prayer that God would bless America.

When we look a little further afield, this trend becomes even more obvious. Dictators have tried to gag Jesus and to convince the world that he is just like them. Frederick the Great of Prussia argued that Jesus was *"the autocrat of the universe"*, and Adolf Hitler told

---

1    Mikhail Gorbachev speaking in the British *Daily Telegraph* on 16th June 1992. Fidel Castro speaking in an article in *Time* magazine on 30th December 1985.

2    John Quincy Adams in a speech at Newburyport, Massachusetts, on 4th July 1837.

his adoring listeners that Jesus had led the *"fight for the world against the Jewish poison… It was for this that he had to shed his blood upon the cross."*[3]

Civil rights activists have tried to gag Jesus too. Florence Nightingale hailed him as a fighter for women's rights, arguing that *"Jesus Christ raised women above the condition of mere slaves."* Malcolm X claimed that *"Christ wasn't white. Christ was black. The poor, brainwashed American Negro has been made to believe that Christ was white to manoeuvre him into worshipping the white man."*[4]

This trend continues unabated today. All around us people are trying to gag Jesus. Muslims claim that Jesus was a Muslim prophet who was simply misunderstood. Self-help gurus tell us that Jesus was the ultimate life coach. I even read an article by a gay rights activist which argued that Jesus' decision to spend three intensive years with twelve male disciples is proof that he was gay. Jesus isn't just the most talked about, sung about, written about and fought about person in world history. He is also the most gagged and kidnapped and hijacked person in world history. Everybody wants to put their own words into Jesus' mouth and to make him say exactly what they want to hear. But more and more people are longing to do away with the background noise and to let the real Jesus do the talking.

---

3    Frederick II of Prussia writing to the French philosopher Voltaire on 19th March 1776. Adolf Hitler in a speech in Munich on 12th April 1922.

4    Florence Nightingale in her essay *Cassandra* (1860). Malcolm X in an interview for *Playboy Magazine* in May 1963.

That's why I think that you will find this short book very helpful. If it is possible to get to know the real Jesus, then we ought to. Nobody is thought about, talked about, written about, blogged about, tweeted about, sung about or ranted about as much as Jesus – and yet nobody is so little understood. Each of us needs to research the life and teachings of the greatest human being who ever lived.

In this book we will strip away the background noise by going back to the four original historical sources for the life of Jesus. Two of Jesus' twelve disciples wrote accounts of the real Jesus as they knew him: we know those books today as the gospels of Matthew and John. Another of Jesus' disciples was an uneducated fisherman named Simon Peter, who asked his more educated friend Mark to write down his account of the life of Jesus in a third gospel. Shortly afterwards, a highly educated Greek doctor from the multiracial city of Antioch turned his hand to investigative journalism and spent two years interviewing all the key eyewitnesses of Jesus' life across the length and breadth of Israel. His historical account is known to us today as the gospel of Luke.

These were men who warned that people would try to gag Jesus in the future. John warned that *"The false Christ is coming, and even now many false Christs have come"*.[5] Their friend Paul warned that *"I am afraid*

---

5    He wrote this in about 95 AD in a letter which forms part of the Bible (1 John 2:18). The Greek word *antichristos* does not mean somebody who is against Christ so much as somebody who is a *false Christ*.

*that just as Eve was deceived by the serpent's cunning, your minds may somehow be led astray from your sincere and pure devotion to Christ. For if someone comes to you and preaches a Jesus other than the Jesus we preached... you put up with it easily enough."*[6]

Matthew was a greedy tax collector until he met the ungagged Jesus. Peter and John were simple fishermen. Luke was a typical pagan. Instead of trying to gag Jesus and to force him to say what they wanted to hear, they had the humility to listen. When they did so, they found that his teaching changed everything. They listened open-mouthed to the fifteen outrageous things which I highlight in this book from Jesus' teachings, and they fell in love with the most controversial figure in the whole of human history.

So get ready to discover the real Jesus of Nazareth for yourself. He isn't bound and gagged any more. He is ready to tell it like it really is to us today.

---

6    He wrote this in a letter in about 55 AD which also forms part of the Bible (2 Corinthians 11:3–4).

# 1

# JESUS ON STRESS

Most people don't find the first of Jesus' ungagged teachings very controversial. That's because they haven't understood it. They think that Jesus' teaching about stress and worry is nothing more than fortune-cookie wisdom, nothing more than a first-century version of the Bobby McFerrin song, "Don't Worry, Be Happy". But it isn't. It is much, much more radical than that. It tells us that stress is the chief symptom of our idolatry and self-worship. When we understand what Jesus said about stress and worry, it's easy to see why it got him killed.

The gospel writers tell us that the issue of stress and worry was a recurring theme in Jesus' teaching.[1] Luke tells us what he taught in the autumn of 29 AD, only five or six months before his enemies crucified him:

---

1    For example, in Matthew 6:25–34; 11:28–30 and in Luke 8:14; 10:38–42; 21:34.

*Do not worry about your life, what you will eat; or about your body, what you will wear. For life is more than food, and the body more than clothes. Consider the ravens: They do not sow or reap, they have no storeroom or barn; yet God feeds them. And how much more valuable you are than birds! Who of you by worrying can add a single hour to your life? Since you cannot do this very little thing, why do you worry about the rest?*

*Consider how the wild flowers grow. They do not labour or spin. Yet I tell you, not even Solomon in all his splendour was dressed like one of these. If that is how God clothes the grass of the field, which is here today, and tomorrow is thrown into the fire, how much more will he clothe you – you of little faith! And do not set your heart on what you will eat or drink; do not worry about it. For the pagan world runs after all such things, and your Father knows that you need them. But seek his kingdom, and these things will be given to you as well. Do not be afraid, little flock, for your Father has been pleased to give you the kingdom.* (Luke 12:22–32)

I live in London. It's a crazy, stressed-out city. In fact, it's a city where people wear their busyness and stress as a badge of honour. When I catch the train to work, none of us are resting. We are part of an army of commuters who all tap away at smartphones and iPads, determined to squeeze the juice out of every single second of the day for sending emails, social networking and, above all, making money. When we get home from work we don't spend the evenings and weekends resting. We cram our free time with so many leisure activities that most of us have to go back to work on Monday to recover.

Things may be a little different where you are, but in my city stress is killing us. Twenty per cent of British workers take time off work due to stress each year,[2] and over 5 million admit that they spend most of their lives "very" or "extremely" stressed.[3] So when Jesus told his disciples not to worry, he wasn't just mouthing pretty platitudes. He was challenging something at the very heart of the way we live our lives.

I want to help you understand what Jesus is telling us here about stress and worry. I want to help you grasp why God sees our overbusyness as a very serious sin, on a par with out-and-out blasphemy. The best way for me to do so is to take you on a journey through three Old Testament passages which provide the background to Jesus' teaching.

The Bible begins with God creating the world. It took him six days, and on the seventh day he rested. Most people who read Genesis assume God rested because he was tired after finishing such a big job, but Jesus tells us that this wasn't why he rested at all: *"My Father is always at his work to this very day, and I too am working"* (John 5:17). He uses the Greek form of the Hebrew word *shābath*, which was used for God resting in Genesis, when he explains that *"The*

---

2    This data comes from a 2010 survey by the UK mental health charity MIND. It found that one in five workers had taken at least one day off work due to stress during the previous year.

3    This data comes from a survey by the UK Health and Safety Executive. It found that British workers take 13.5 million days a year off work due to stress, costing the economy £3.7 billion.

*Sabbath was made for humankind"* (Mark 2:27). Jesus tells us that God rested for Adam's sake, not his own, because day seven for him was day one for Adam. He had created a human being who needed to stop each day for mealtimes and for sleep,[4] and he wanted to teach him from the outset to relax in a garden he hadn't planted, to enjoy animals he hadn't made and to eat fruit he hadn't grown. In short, he wanted him to grasp that God is God and we are not. Adam never knew what stress was until he decided to have a go at being God himself and was cursed with *"painful toil"* and with survival by *"the sweat of your brow"*.[5] Adam had rejected God's Paradise and had chosen a life of stress and worry instead.

Fast-forward several centuries and we discover in Genesis 6:11 that people continued to make this same choice. It describes their sin as *hāmās*, a Hebrew word which is usually translated *violence* (as in the name of the Palestinian terrorist organization) but which essentially refers to *busy self-assertiveness*. Jesus describes the overbusyness of that generation when he tells us that *"People were eating, drinking, marrying and being given in marriage up to the day Noah entered the ark"* (Luke 17:27). God saved Noah because he was totally different in his outlook. He emerged from the ark after the Flood with the mother of all to-do lists: He was in charge of the rebuilding of civilization. Yet

---

4    Psalm 121 encourages us to treat our need for sleep as a nightly reminder that God is God and we are not.

5    Genesis 3:17–19. We discover in Genesis 3:5 that the essence of Adam's sin was trying to be like God.

the first item which he placed at the top of his to-do list in Genesis 8 was to kneel down and worship God, resting on his knees before his Creator.

Fast-forward a few more centuries and we find that Moses constantly reminded the Israelites that God is God and we are not. When they panicked at the Red Sea, he assured them that *"The Lord will fight for you; you need only to be still"* (Exodus 14:14). He gave them God's command at Mount Sinai to take one day in seven as a day of rest because *"This will be a sign between me and you for the generations to come, so you may know that I am the Lord"* (Exodus 31:13). He warned them that if they failed to rest then they would suffer from burnout and exhaustion (Leviticus 26:2–35), and when he caught an Israelite working on the Sabbath he didn't let him off with a simple caution. When we get offended that he ordered the Sabbath-breaker's execution in Numbers 15, we simply show we haven't understood Jesus' teaching about stress and worry. We haven't grasped that *"I'm worried"* is just another way of saying *"I'm not convinced that God will do his job without me"*, or that *"I'm feeling stressed"* is just another way of saying *"I'm trying to do God's job for him and it's not working out for me."* Jesus warns that stress and worry aren't minor vices or personality flaws. They are the symptoms of our self-worship.[6]

In Luke 12, Jesus lists some of the biggest things we worry about – things like money and food and clothes

---

6    The Hebrew Law reserved the death penalty for very few things: mainly for murder, idolatry and blasphemy. The Sabbath-breaker was executed for acting as though he was his own little god.

and our health – and then tells us that "*the pagan world runs after all such things*". People who don't know God get very stressed about these things because they live their lives as little gods and therefore feel the burden of providing for themselves. God hands them over to their stress and worry in order that every bird and flower will preach a sermon to them about God's provision. In cities like mine, where people can't stop checking their emails for an evening, let alone one day in seven, God uses stress and worry to warn us to stop blaspheming and to start sabbathing. The fourth-century writer Hilary of Poitiers described stress and worry as "*a blasphemous anxiety to do God's work for him*".[7] He understood the message of Psalm 46:10: "*Be still, and know that I am God.*"

Many of the people who heard Jesus saying this were furious. Since money was the currency of their attempts to play at God, they persuaded one of Jesus' twelve disciples to betray him for a handful of silver coins. While he waited for them to come and arrest him in the Garden of Gethsemane, Jesus sweated drops of blood from his brow in fulfilment of the curse which had fallen on Adam for attempting to be like God (Luke 22:44). He was crucified wearing a crown of thorns on his forehead because thorns and brambles were the symbol of Adam's painful labour in Genesis 3. While the merchants of Jerusalem were busy with their trading, while the priests of Jerusalem were busy with their religion, and while the homeowners of

7    Hilary of Poitiers writing in about 360 AD in his treatise *On the Trinity* (4.6).

Jerusalem were busy with their shopping and cleaning and cooking, Jesus died on a wooden cross for their sin and cried out, *"It is finished!"* (John 19:30). He has paid the penalty for our blasphemous anxiety to do God's work for him. We don't have to earn our forgiveness. We simply have to rest in what the Lord has achieved for us.

You can tell whether you are following the real Jesus or a Jesus of your own making by the way that you respond to this as the first of Jesus' fifteen offensive teachings. Will you get upset and resist him or will you surrender to him? Will you confess your overbusyness and your blasphemous anxiety to do God's work for him? If you will, then Jesus promises that your painful toil is over: *"The work of God is this: to believe in the one he has sent"* (John 6:29).

Once forgiven, will you adopt a new lifestyle which plays by a different set of rules in the midst of a stressed-out and burned-out culture? Will you trust God to be God and simply be content to be his creature? Will you let him carry the weight of your life and trust him like a little child? If you will, then Jesus promises to deliver you from stress and worry:

> *Come to me, all you who are weary and burdened, and I will give you rest. Take my yoke upon you and learn from me, for I am gentle and humble in heart, and you will find rest for your souls. For my yoke is easy and my burden is light.* (Matthew 11:28–30)

# 2

# JESUS ON FORGIVENESS

Yoshinori Yamaguchi straightened his flying jacket. He felt proud to have been selected to serve as a kamikaze pilot. He and his friends had volunteered to play their part in Captain Okamura's plan to turn the tide of World War Two in its final year through suicide attacks on American and British ships. *"In our present situation I firmly believe that the only way to swing the war in our favour is to resort to crash-dive tactics with our planes,"* the captain had boasted on the radio. *"Provide me with 300 planes and I will turn the tide of war."*[1] Over twice as many young Japanese men had volunteered for these suicide missions as were required.

Yoshinori Yamaguchi could just see the USS Essex in the distance as he adjusted his flying jacket one last time. It was 25th November 1944 and he had well over 100 kilograms of high explosives stowed in his Yokusuka D4Y dive bomber. He felt excited that he

---

1    Quoted by Rikihei Inoguchi in *The Divine Wind: Japan's Kamikaze Force in World War II* (1958).

was going to strike a mighty blow for the Japanese Empire, and as he hit the deck of the USS *Essex* he shouted *"Hissatsu!"* at the top of his lungs, which is Japanese for *"Kill without fail!"* Now hold that picture of an exploding Japanese plane in your mind. Jesus tells us it's what we are like whenever we refuse to forgive anybody.

The truth is that Yoshinori Yamaguchi's action backfired. He hardly hurt the Americans at all. He at least hit the ship, which many kamikaze pilots didn't, but he missed the planes on the flight deck and destroyed an empty hangar. The USS *Essex* was not put out of action and it went on to play a key role in the defeat of Japan the following year. Yoshinori Yamaguchi's attack looked impressive but in reality it hurt Japan far more than it did America. He traded his life and his training and his plane in exchange for practically nothing, and Jesus wants us to understand that when we refuse to forgive others it's the same. The only person we end up damaging is ourselves. We are told in Matthew 18:21–35 that

> *Peter came to Jesus and asked, "Lord, how many times shall I forgive my brother or sister who sins against me? Up to seven times?" Jesus answered, "I tell you, not seven times, but seventy-seven times.*
>
> *"Therefore, the kingdom of heaven is like a king who wanted to settle accounts with his servants. As he began the settlement, a man who owed him ten thousand talents was brought to him. Since he was not able to pay, the master ordered that he and his wife*

*and his children and all that he had be sold to repay the
debt. At this the servant fell on his knees before him.
'Be patient with me,' he begged, 'and I will pay back
everything.' The servant's master took pity on him,
cancelled the debt and let him go.*

*"But when that servant went out, he found one of
his fellow servants who owed him a hundred denarii.
He grabbed him and began to choke him. 'Pay back
what you owe me!' he demanded. His fellow servant
fell to his knees and begged him, 'Be patient with me,
and I will pay it back.' But he refused. Instead, he went
off and had the man thrown into prison until he could
pay the debt. When the other servants saw what had
happened, they were outraged and went and told their
master everything that had happened.*

*"Then the master called the servant in. 'You wicked
servant,' he said, 'I cancelled all that debt of yours
because you begged me to. Shouldn't you have had
mercy on your fellow servant just as I had on you?' In
anger his master handed him over to the jailers to be
tortured, until he should pay back all he owed. This is
how my heavenly Father will treat each of you unless
you forgive your brother or sister from your heart."*

Everybody loves to hear Jesus telling them that their
sins will be forgiven. Most of us are like the German
poet Heinrich Heine, who boasted on his death bed
that *"Of course God will forgive me: that's his job."*[2] We
like it rather less, however, when Jesus tells us that

---

2    Sigmund Freud recounts Heine's deathbed words in *The Joke
and Its Relation to the Unconscious* (1905).

unless we forgive others God will not forgive us at all. We protest that such a demand is unreasonable, unjust and impossible. If you have ever been horribly wronged by somebody, then you will understand why people have always tried to gag Jesus when he talks about forgiveness.

Jesus tells us that how we forgive others is the true proof of *how we view ourselves*. He doesn't tell us that the second servant's debt was trifling – 100 denarii was three or four months' salary. Jesus simply points out that it was nothing compared to how much the first servant owed his master – 10,000 talents was 200,000 years' salary! The servant's offer to repay the debt in instalments was preposterous, rather like our attempts to impress God through church attendance or Bible reading, which is why the master interrupts him and offers him mercy instead. He is angry with the servant later because his refusal to forgive a far smaller debt proved he hadn't grasped how serious his own debt had been. He hadn't understood how much it cost his master to wipe the slate clean. Jesus tells us that when we refuse to forgive others it also demonstrates that, deep down, we don't think our sin is very serious and that it didn't cost God very much to forgive it.

Jesus tells us that how we forgive others is the true proof of *how we view God*. Peter expected Jesus to be impressed by his offer to forgive people seven times, since most rabbis taught that revenge was acceptable so long as it was proportionate to the crime: *"Eye for eye, and tooth for tooth"* (Matthew 5:38). He didn't expect Jesus to rebuke him for counting other people's wrongs against him at all, like Hillary Clinton when she remarked that *"They asked Jesus how many times you should forgive, and he said seventy times seven. Well, I want you all to know that I'm keeping a chart."*[3] Instead, Jesus warns us that those who count other people's sins against them are trying to play judge instead of God.[4] Unforgiveness couldn't be more serious.

Jesus isn't telling us in this parable that forgiving others earns forgiveness for ourselves. The master paid the price to forgive the first servant as an act of mercy. He picked up the bill for the servant's crippling debt, just as Jesus did when he laid down his life to pay the penalty for our sin, wronged far more deeply than we will ever be and yet crying out as he died, *"Father, forgive them"* (Luke 23:34). Those who understand this Gospel message naturally forgive others. Those who refuse to forgive others prove that they haven't understood the Gospel message at all.

One of the most painful experiences of my adult life has been watching one of my best friends destroy his life through unforgiveness. He knew that Jesus

3    Hillary Clinton said this at the National Prayer Luncheon in May 1994. Jesus' words in Greek can either be translated *seventy-seven times* or *seventy times seven times*. What matters is not the number but our attitude.
4    Paul tells us in Romans 12:19–21 that when we forgive we actually make room for God to judge wrongdoing, because we get out of the way of his divine justice.

told his followers to *"Forgive us our debts, as we also have forgiven our debtors"* (Matthew 6:12). He knew that Jesus followed this up with a warning that *"if you forgive other people when they sin against you, your heavenly Father will also forgive you. But if you do not forgive others their sins, your Father will not forgive your sins"* (Matthew 6:14–15). Nevertheless, when he discovered that his wife was having an affair, he decided to punish her with bitterness and unforgiveness. While she asked for forgiveness and tried to save their marriage, he chose the path of misery and torture which Jesus describes at the end of the story: *"His master handed him over to the jailers to be tortured, until he should pay back all he owed."* It is impossible to ask the Lord for mercy with one breath while demanding justice and retribution against somebody else with the next.

Thankfully, Jesus tells us that this tiny taste of hell is designed to draw us back to a place of mercy. My friend's unforgiveness has cost him his marriage but he is waking up to the fact that, just like Yoshinori Yamaguchi in his dive bomber, the person who is most hurt by unforgiveness is ourselves. He is slowly becoming like Nelson Mandela when he was released from twenty-seven unjust years in prison and refused to use his influence to take vengeance on his white enemies. *"Resentment is like drinking poison and then hoping it will kill your enemies,"* he insisted as he led a divided nation on a pathway to healing. My prayer is that the torture of my friend's bitterness will eventually teach him to walk a similar road.

I know that forgiveness is easier to admire than it is to copy, so don't miss the fact that Jesus promises to help you to *"forgive your brother or sister from your heart."* When he bore the penalty for your sin on the cross, he also bore your pain so that you need not bear it any longer. He died as the victim of injustice so that he can help you to pray with him: *"Lord, do not hold this sin against them."*[5]

He will help you to forgive like Corrie ten Boom, a survivor of the Nazi death camps during World War Two. She describes the moment when God helped her to forgive one of her prison guards, in spite of his involvement in the death of her father and sister, when she met him after the war:

> *I tried to smile, I struggled to raise my hand. I could not. I felt nothing, not the slightest spark of warmth or charity. And so again I breathed a silent prayer. Jesus, I cannot forgive him. Give me your forgiveness. As I took his hand the most incredible thing happened. From my shoulder along my arm and through my hand a current seemed to pass from me to him, while into my heart sprang a love for this stranger that almost overwhelmed me.*
>
> *And so I discovered that it is not on our forgiveness any more than on our goodness that the world's*

---

5    Stephen prays this in Acts 7:60 as an example of how Jesus can empower us to forgive our enemies.

*healing hinges, but on his. When he tells us to love our enemies, he gives, along with the command, the love itself.*[6]

So forgive. Forgive because unforgiveness is spiritual suicide. Forgive because Jesus first forgave you. Forgive because he promises to help you do so if you will let him. Forgive because, unless you forgive others, Jesus says that God will not forgive you.

---

6    Corrie ten Boom recalls this breakthrough in forgiveness in her book *The Hiding Place* (1971).

# 3

# JESUS ON POSSESSIONS

Buying this book about the ungagged Jesus didn't cost you very much. Doing what Jesus says in it will cost you everything. That's what people always find when they let the real Jesus do the talking.

The bound-and-gagged Jesus promises you prosperity. He behaves at dinner parties and sympathizes with your concern about house prices, interest rates and the rising cost of fuel. He is far too polite to mention money, but the real Jesus isn't. He spoke more about money than about heaven and hell combined. He tells us that how we spend our money is the truest gauge of what we really think of his teaching. He tells us that the clearest statement of faith is a person's bank statement.

Giovanni Francesco di Bernardone was a prosperous Italian playboy until he read Jesus' teaching in Mark 10:17–30. He was the son of a wealthy cloth merchant and about to inherit a small fortune from his father, when he started reading the family Bible:

*As Jesus started on his way, a man ran up to him and fell on his knees before him. "Good teacher," he asked, "what must I do to inherit eternal life?" "Why do you call me good?" Jesus answered. "No one is good – except God alone. You know the commandments: 'You shall not murder, you shall not commit adultery, you shall not steal, you shall not give false testimony, you shall not defraud, honour your father and mother.'*

*"Teacher," he declared, "all these I have kept since I was a boy." Jesus looked at him and loved him. "One thing you lack," he said. "Go, sell everything you have and give to the poor, and you will have treasure in heaven. Then come, follow me." At this the man's face fell. He went away sad, because he had great wealth.*

*Jesus looked around and said to his disciples, "How hard it is for the rich to enter the kingdom of God!" The disciples were amazed at his words. But Jesus said again, "Children, how hard it is to enter the kingdom of God! It is easier for a camel to go through the eye of a needle than for someone who is rich to enter the kingdom of God." The disciples were even more amazed, and said to each other, "Who then can be saved?" Jesus looked at them and said, "With man this is impossible, but not with God; all things are possible with God."*

*Then Peter spoke up, "We have left everything to follow you!" "Truly I tell you," Jesus replied, "no one who has left home or brothers or sisters or mother or father or children or fields for me and the gospel will fail to receive a hundred times as much in this present age: homes, brothers, sisters, mothers, children and*

*fields – along with persecutions – and in the age to
come eternal life."*

Giovanni Francesco di Bernardone was so convicted by
the gulf between Jesus' teaching and his own lifestyle
that he sold the contents of his father's warehouse and
gave the proceeds away. When his father dragged him
to court and threatened to disinherit him of everything
except for the clothes he was wearing unless he
apologized, he stripped down to his underwear in the
courtroom and walked barefoot into the snowy streets
outside. Giovanni Francesco di Bernardone is better
known to us as Francis of Assisi, the founder of an
order of monks who gave away everything to follow
Jesus and who still inspire millions of people around
the world today.

Seven hundred years later, a star of the England
cricket team read these same verses in Mark 10. Charles
T. Studd was captain of the Cambridge University
cricket team and the only English batsman left at the
crease when Australia beat England for the first time
on English soil in the infamous match which gave
rise to The Ashes series. That same year, he became,
effectively, British sports personality of the year. He
was fabulously wealthy and extremely famous. Then
he started listening to the ungagged Jesus.

Charles T. Studd was convicted by Jesus' words
to the rich young ruler that his privileged lifestyle
was very sinful. It was normal by the standards of
Victorian Britain, but he knew it wasn't the lifestyle

of a follower of Christ. He reflected later that *"Either I had to be a thief and keep what wasn't mine, or else I had to give up everything to God. When I came to see that Jesus Christ had died for me, it didn't seem hard to give up all for him."* He gave away 90 per cent of his family fortune to fund missionaries and orphanages, holding back a mere 10 per cent to help him set up home when he got married. When his fiancée Priscilla read these verses, she refused even this: *"Charlie, what did the Lord tell the rich young man to do? Sell all. Well then, we will start clear with the Lord at our wedding."*[1] The British sports personality of the year left for China with only five pounds in his pocket and died almost fifty years later as a missionary in an obscure village 4,000 miles away from home.

It's easy to see why people want to gag Jesus. The real Jesus is expensive. We marshal reasons why these verses don't actually apply to you and me – they are just for the rich young ruler or for medieval playboys or for Victorian cricketers. That's why we need to be honest with ourselves about four general statements in this passage which apply to each one of us. They may not mean stripping down to our underwear, but they will require a radical response of our own.

First, Jesus talks about possessions *because he loves us.* Mark 10 tells us that *"Jesus looked at him and loved him."* God isn't in need of our handouts. He wants us to give him our possessions because he knows that it will do us good. The French author André Gide

---

1    The quotes in this chapter come from Norman Grubb's biography *C.T. Studd: Cricketer and Pioneer* (1933).

observed that "*Complete possession is proved only by giving. All you are unable to give possesses you.*"[2] Jesus doesn't talk about money in order to back us into a corner. He talks about money to set us free.

Second, Jesus talks about possessions *because they make us self-sufficient*. The rich young ruler addresses Jesus as "*good teacher*" because that is all he thinks he needs Jesus to be. Even when Jesus recites the Ten Commandments and challenges him that no one is good except God alone, he still can't see how much he needs a Saviour. Jesus tells him to give away his possessions so that he will get into the habit of looking to God each day for provision and forgiveness and salvation. Rich people can rely on God (like Joseph of Arimathea in Matthew 27:57), but Jesus tells us that such faith is rare. He tells each of us to give away enough of our possessions so that we can no longer be self-sufficient.

Jesus tells us that we ought to give away more than generous unbelievers (Matthew 5:20 and 23:23), but his emphasis here and in Luke 21:1–4 is not so much on how we give as it is on how much we have left over. Unless what we give away devastates our standard of living and throws us onto God's mercy daily, then we aren't giving enough away.

Third, Jesus talks about possessions *because they can distract us*. The rich young ruler's problem was that he was straitjacketed by his fortune. He could afford whatever he wanted but he couldn't afford to give it all away. Peter left his fishing business to follow Jesus.

---

2    André Gide in *New Fruits of the Earth* (1935).

Matthew left a table piled high with Roman coins. Zacchaeus promised that *"Here and now I give half of my possessions to the poor, and if I have cheated anybody out of anything, I will pay back four times the amount."*[3] But the rich young ruler went away sad. People who follow the real Jesus keep their focus on what matters and take radical steps to prevent their possessions from distracting them. They have the same spirit which made Charles T. Studd explain to sports fans: *"I knew that cricket would not last, and honour would not last, and nothing in this world would last, but it was worthwhile living for the world to come… If Jesus Christ be God and died for me, then no sacrifice can be too great for me to make for him."*

Fourth, Jesus talks about possessions *because they can make us poor*. When Peter complains about how much he has given away, Jesus reminds him that God views our gifts as an investment in his goodness, and that he will reward us both in this age and in the age to come. Charles T. Studd reflected on this passage towards the end of his life and concluded that

> *God has promised to give a hundredfold for everything we give to him. A hundredfold is a wonderful percentage; it is ten thousand per cent. God began to give me back the hundredfold wonderfully quick. Not long after this I was sent down to Shanghai… When I saw that brother right soundly converted I said, "This is ten thousand per cent and more"… What is it worth*

---

3    Luke 19:8. This response to the Gospel was not exceptional, since we read that many other Christians responded the same way as him in Acts 2:44–45 and 4:34–35.

*to possess the riches of the world, when a man comes
to face eternity?... I have tasted most of the pleasures
that the world can give. I do not suppose there was one
that I had not experienced; but I can tell you that these
pleasures were as nothing compared to the joy that the
saving of that one soul gave me.*

Jesus therefore warns you to view your possessions
as potential enemies in your own home. They can
possess you, they can distract you, they can drive you
away from God, and they can therefore impoverish
you. Jesus urges you to treat your earthly riches as
mere pocket money, given to you by your heavenly
Father in order to train you to handle the true riches
of heaven.

So let's give away our money and possessions
for the sake of God's Kingdom. Let's give away so
much that our lifestyle is seriously affected. Let's give
until we feel alarmed at the thought of how much
this means we are going to have to rely on God each
day. Let's give like Francis of Assisi and like Charles
T. Studd, and let's dedicate whatever possessions we
have left to the one who gave up his life so that he
could set us free.

# JESUS ON PORNOGRAPHY AND MASTURBATION

Osama Bin Laden wanted the world to view him as a champion of Islamic purity against the wicked and depraved influence of America. *"We fought with you because we are free and we don't put up with transgressions,"* he fumed in one of his videotape broadcasts. Yet when he was located and killed by a team of US Navy Seals at his hideout in Pakistan in May 2011, they found an extensive stash of pornography on his computer.[1] What people are in public is often different from what they are in private.

Martin McVeigh was an unknown Roman Catholic priest in Northern Ireland until he ran a first communion class at his local primary school in March

---

1    This video was broadcast on Al-Jazeera and CNN on 29th October 2004. Although some have claimed that the pornography was put on his computer by the US to discredit him, Google data reveals that Pakistan outranks every other country in the world when it comes to internet searches for pornography.

2012. When he inserted his USB stick into the laptop in order to start his presentation, he didn't realize that Windows AutoPlay was enabled on the computer. The horrified children and parents were presented, not with a lecture on communion, but with a slideshow of gay pornography. Father McVeigh protested his innocence but his bishop immediately relieved him of his duties.

In many ways, neither of these two revelations on opposite sides of the world should surprise us. We all know that pornography is big business and that its use is very widespread. What is surprising is that we get so offended that Jesus should dare to teach about pornography and masturbation – as if what people do in the comfort of their own homes should be of no concern to God. Jesus told his disciples:

> *You have heard that it was said, "You shall not commit adultery." But I tell you that anyone who looks at a woman lustfully has already committed adultery with her in his heart. If your right eye causes you to stumble, gouge it out and throw it away. It is better for you to lose one part of your body than for your whole body to be thrown into hell. And if your right hand causes you to stumble, cut it off and throw it away. It is better for you to lose one part of your body than for your whole body to go into hell.* (Matthew 5:27–30)

If you don't feel at least slightly offended by Jesus' teaching in these verses, then you probably aren't reading them properly. He doesn't buy the line that what we do in the privacy of our own homes doesn't matter, just so long as it doesn't harm anybody else. He tells us that what we do with our eyes and our hands really matters to God. In fact, he says God takes this issue so seriously that it places us in danger of hellfire.[2]

Jesus starts by telling us that we are all sexual sinners. It didn't matter that most of his original listeners had never broken the Seventh Commandment by committing adultery. They had all looked lustfully at men or women, so they had all committed adultery in their hearts. They had all rebelled against God's command to keep sexual enjoyment within the holy boundaries of marriage – they just hadn't turned their wicked thoughts into wicked actions. They may have let their eyes linger on another person's body (the fact that a third of visitors to adult entertainment websites are female suggests that this is twice as big a problem for men as it is for women[3]). They may have fantasized emotionally in their hearts and, since the Greek word for *lust* in this passage is *epithumeō*, which simply means *to desire strongly*, this describes a problem which is just as big for women as it is for men. E.L. James aimed at a female audience with her erotic sadomasochistic novel *Fifty Shades of Grey*, and it became the fastest-selling paperback of all time within months of its publication in 2011. She played on the fact that women express their strong desires differently,

---

2    Jesus' teaching on hell is so offensive that I will devote a whole chapter to it later on.

3    This data comes from a Nielsen/NetRatings report in 2009.

through erotic fiction and flirtation and daydreaming about what it would be like to be married to someone else instead. Jesus makes it clear that every single one of us has broken the Seventh Commandment.

As if this wasn't enough, Jesus then goes one step further. It doesn't require much imagination to grasp what he is saying. He moves from frank talk about lusting with our eyes into frank talk about sinning with our right hands. He doesn't need to use the word to make it clear that he is talking about masturbation. We live in a culture where Jerry Seinfeld claims that this is simply a normal part of being male: *"We have to do it. It's part of our lifestyle. It's like, er, shaving."*[4] Jesus cuts across our culture by telling us – male or female – that God takes our sexual purity so seriously that it would be better for us to lose our right hands than to lose everything in hell.

Are you offended yet? Most people are when they stop gagging Jesus and start listening to him for a moment on pornography and masturbation. They ask who Jesus thinks he is to talk to them this way. Matthew was hoping that you would ask.

Matthew wants you to grasp that Jesus was a *man*, and a single man at that. He knew exactly what it is like to be a red-blooded single male. Jesus was an oddball in his culture, since he was aged over thirty and still single, so he had actually been tempted more than any of his married listeners in the area of lust and had resisted the temptation every time.[5] Hebrews 4:15

---

4    *Seinfeld*, Season 4, Episode 11 – "The Contest" (1992).

5    We can tell that most of the disciples were married, because

tells us that *"we have one who has been tempted in every way, just as we are – yet he did not sin."* Jesus doesn't talk to us about pornography and masturbation because he doesn't understand the problem. He talks to us both as a red-blooded male and as a sexually sinless virgin because he wants to set us free.

Matthew also wants you to grasp that Jesus is *God,* and that he has a right to talk to you about sexual sin because he created sex and gave it to you as a precious gift to treasure. He gave sex to men and women in order to draw husbands and wives together, so he doesn't view it as a private matter when we use his gift in a way which tears people apart. He sees very clearly what the feminist author Naomi Wolf only grasped quite lately when she wrote that *"In the end, porn doesn't whet men's appetites – it turns them off the real thing,"* and that *"young women are worrying that as mere flesh and blood, they can scarcely get, let alone hold, their attention."*[6] Jesus isn't as content as we are with a culture in which young girls dress up sexually, middle-aged women feel unpretty and wives feel unloved because they know they can't compete on looks with the other women in their home. Jesus isn't afraid to point out that pornography and masturbation leave men frustrated in their marriages instead of delighting in their wives.

---

Peter had a mother-in-law (Matthew 8:14) and Jesus promised them a reward for having left behind their *children* to follow him (Mark 10:29–30).

6    Naomi Wolf is the author of the best-selling book *The Beauty Myth* (1991). She said this in an article in *New York* magazine on 20th October 2003.

Matthew also wants you to grasp that Jesus is *the sacrifice for your sin*. That's why it's so tragic when people try to gag him, because he died for adulterers, for terrible flirts, for porn addicts, for masturbators and for you. If you confess you are a sexual sinner, then he promises to forgive you because he perfectly fulfilled this passage. The one who tells us to cut off our right hands if they cause us to sin is also the one who stretched out both his hands to be hammered to a cross for our sexual sin. He doesn't tell us to sort out our lives and then come to him with pure hands. He forgives us upfront through an act of undeserved mercy and then asks us to put our dirty hands in his.

Matthew also wants you to grasp that Jesus is your *Deliverer from temptation*. Having forgiven you, he also promises to free you from your sin. That's why he warns us to get radical with our eyes in this passage, because *"The eye is the lamp of the body. If your eyes are healthy, your whole body will be full of light. But if your eyes are unhealthy, your whole body will be full of darkness"* (Matthew 6:22–23). If you went to a restaurant and found lipstick on your glass, several hairs on your plate and dirt on your knife, you would instantly complain. Jesus therefore tells you to be at least as fussy about what goes into your heart through your eyes. Easier than gouging out eyes and cutting off hands is cutting off your internet connection for a while, or cutting out an unhelpful friendship, or cutting out certain books and magazines and movies. Easier than cutting off hands is using your remote control to change channel because you have made a covenant with your eyes not to look at images which excite lust (Job 31:1). Easier than gouging out eyes is using your eyelids as a mighty weapon in the spiritual fight, closing them every time you see a suggestive image on a poster or at the movies.

Finally, Matthew wants you to grasp that Jesus is *our deepest source of satisfaction*, whether you are a man or a woman, married or single, young or old. He wants you to remember that the New Testament describes Jesus as the Bridegroom and tells you he is coming back to be united with his People as a pure and spotless Bride. Thoughts like this one stirred the nineteenth-century Scottish preacher Thomas Chalmers to urge his hearers to rid their minds of sinful thoughts by filling them with pure thoughts of Jesus Christ instead: *"Such is the grasping tendency of the human heart that it must have a something to lay hold of... The only way to dispossess it of an old affection is by the expulsive power of a new one."*[7] Lustful thoughts find it easy to fill a vacuum but they cannot live in a heart which is fully captivated by the beauty of Jesus.

So don't be surprised that Jesus talks freely about pornography and masturbation. He does so because he is your Saviour and Deliverer. He wants to forgive you and to teach you to walk the path of sexual purity as you follow him every day.

---

7    He said this in a sermon on 1 John 2:15 entitled "The Expulsive Power of a New Affection".

# 5

# JESUS ON ANGER

When most of us think of anger, we tend to think of people like Liam Gallagher. It's ironic that the lead singer of Oasis who had a number-one hit with "Don't Look Back in Anger" is famous for his outbursts of anger and rage. He has fallen out with his agents, with his wife, with his brother Noel, with fellow musicians and with his fans. Noel Gallagher told *Q Magazine* in an interview in April 2009 that *"Liam is the angriest man you'll ever meet. He's like a man with a fork in a world of soup."*

Even if you were never a fan of Oasis, you are unlikely to think of anger as a good thing. Anyone who grew up on the classic TV series *The Incredible Hulk* will remember Bruce Banner's famous line in the opening credits: *"Don't make me angry. You wouldn't like me when I'm angry."* Whenever Bruce Banner gets angry he turns into the Hulk and goes on a rampage which makes Liam Gallagher look like a UN peacekeeper.

Few people try to gag Jesus when he condemns this kind of anger because its damaging effects are so easy to see. If you struggle with anger towards your husband or your wife, towards your parents or your children, towards an employer or the government, this may be all that Jesus wants to say to you today about anger: *"You have heard that it was said to the people long ago, 'You shall not murder, and anyone who murders will be subject to judgment.' But I tell you that anyone who is angry with a brother or sister will be subject to judgment"* (Matthew 5:21–22). It's very similar to what Jesus said in the previous chapter about adultery. Lusting in our hearts is a form of adultery, coveting in our hearts is a form of theft, and getting angry towards someone in our hearts is a form of murder.

For most of us, however, this isn't all that Jesus has to say on anger. He wants to warn most of us that our bigger problem is that we don't get angry enough about the right things. The gagged-and-bound Jesus never talks about this kind of anger. He is so watered-down, so toothless, so mild mannered and so dreadfully apologetic that he wouldn't have it in him to make either waves or enemies. The real Jesus, on the other hand, got very angry when he saw injustice and prejudice and rebellion against God. Of course he wants to warn us against getting angry like Liam Gallagher or the Incredible Hulk, but he also wants to stir us to feel anger of the righteous kind:

*When it was almost time for the Jewish Passover, Jesus went up to Jerusalem. In the temple courts he found people selling cattle, sheep and doves, and others sitting*

*at tables exchanging money. So he made a whip out of
cords, and drove all from the temple courts, both sheep
and cattle; he scattered the coins of the money changers
and overturned their tables. To those who sold doves he
said, "Get these out of here! Stop turning my Father's
house into a market!" His disciples remembered that
it is written: "Zeal for your house will consume me."*
(John 2:13–17)

This was not an isolated episode in the life of Jesus.
He cleared the temple courts two years later when he
again got angry at people profiteering from religion,
and he got just as angry in one of the synagogues when
the Jewish leaders put their man-made rules ahead of
helping a man who was in terrible distress:

*Another time Jesus went into the synagogue, and a
man with a shrivelled hand was there. Some of them
were looking for a reason to accuse Jesus, so they
watched him closely to see if he would heal him on the
Sabbath. Jesus said to the man with the shrivelled hand,
"Stand up in front of everyone." Then Jesus asked
them, "Which is lawful on the Sabbath: to do good or
to do evil, to save life or to kill?" But they remained
silent. He looked around at them in anger and, deeply
distressed at their stubborn hearts, said to the man,
"Stretch out your hand." He stretched it out, and his
hand was completely restored. Then the Pharisees went
out and began to plot with the Herodians how they
might kill Jesus.* (Mark 3:1–6)

The Jesus who is preached in many churches today wouldn't provoke anybody to plot how they might kill him. He is far too respectable and easygoing to pose a threat to anyone. If the Jesus you have heard about would not get angry enough to clear the temple courts with a whip like Indiana Jones, and if he would not provoke people to silence him at any cost, then you might not have heard about the real Jesus at all.

When the German theologians of the early twentieth century gagged Jesus on this issue, it quickly spelt disaster. Adolf von Harnack led a movement that questioned whether Jesus truly spoke any of his most offensive teaching and whether he performed any miracles at all. The movement's man-made Jesus started looking more and more like an early-twentieth-century German. Von Harnack signed a public statement which endorsed the Kaiser's war aims at the start of World War One, and he created a theology which made it easy for the German church to tolerate Adolf Hitler and the Nazis. A German pastor named Dietrich Bonhoeffer swam against the tide when he preached the ungagged Jesus and his anger towards the injustice of the Nazi regime: *"We have been silent witnesses of evil deeds: we have been drenched by many storms; we have learnt the arts of equivocation and pretence... Silence in the face of evil is itself evil: God will not hold us guiltless. Not to speak is to speak. Not to act is to act."*[1] Bonhoeffer was arrested by the Nazis for an act of righteous anger, stripped naked and hanged in the last days of the War.

---

1    This is a combination of two quotes, the first of which comes from a letter to his friends in January 1943.

Nevertheless, Jesus demonstrates that such righteous anger pleases God. Hebrews 1:9 tells us that God the Father was delighted by Jesus' anger because it showed that *"You have loved righteousness and hated wickedness"*. Jesus told us to react in the same way to the evil and injustice in the world, even though it will make people willing to do anything to silence us: *"Do not suppose that I have come to bring peace to the earth. I did not come to bring peace, but a sword,"* he warned his followers in Matthew 10:34. Kaj Munk was a church leader who echoed Bonhoeffer's righteous anger against the Nazis in occupied Denmark. Just before he was killed by the Gestapo in January 1944, he preached that

> *What we Christians lack is not psychology or literature… We lack a holy rage – the recklessness which comes from the knowledge of God and humanity. The ability to rage when justice lies prostrate on the streets, and when the lie rages across the face of the earth… a holy anger about the things that are wrong in the world. To rage against the ravaging of God's earth, and the destruction of God's world. To rage when little children must die of hunger, when the tables of the rich are sagging with food. To rage at the senseless killing of so many, and against the madness of militaries. To rage at the lie that calls the threat of death and the strategy of destruction peace. To rage against complacency.*[2]

So what is the difference between the righteous anger of Jesus and Dietrich Bonhoeffer and Kaj Munk and the unrighteous anger of Liam Gallagher and the

---

2    Quoted by Shane Claiborne in *The Irresistible Revolution* (2006).

Incredible Hulk? It's absolutely vital that we ask ourselves this question because our deceitful hearts will always try to trick us that our anger is perfectly justified. As we study the life of the ungagged Jesus, we find three principles which help us to determine whether our anger is righteous or sinful.

First, Jesus shows us that righteous anger is always self-controlled. Did you notice that John told us that when Jesus saw people profiteering in the temple courts he went off and *"made a whip out of cords"*? He didn't lash out with whatever weapon was at hand because he held his anger under control. The second time he drove the traders out of the temple courts, Mark 11 tells us that he took a night to sleep on the problem before acting. This reminds us of 1 Samuel 15:11, which tells us that *"Samuel was angry, and he cried out to the Lord all that night."* If you want to know whether your anger is righteous or sinful, take a night to pray and sleep on it before acting in the morning.

Second, Jesus shows us that righteous anger is always against evil and not against people. John seems to suggest that Jesus used his whip on the sheep and cattle rather than on the traders when he drove them out of the temple courts. Mark 3 tells us that he was infuriated by the Jewish leaders but channelled his anger into healing the man rather than into fighting with the Pharisees. Righteous anger attacks the work of the Devil through people rather than the people themselves. Archbishop Desmond Tutu modelled this when he led Christians in the angry fight against apartheid in South Africa rather than against the white oppressors themselves, explaining that *"There are things that must evoke our anger to show we care. It is what we do with that anger. If we direct that energy we can use it positively or destructively."*[3]

Third, Jesus shows us that righteous anger always seeks for the will of God to be done in the world. The word "sin" has "I" in the middle, and so does sinful anger. It always flares up when *my* desires, *my* needs and *my* ambitions are thwarted, because it always seeks to satisfy self. Jesus' anger was caused by zeal for God's house in John 2 and by the Pharisees' stubborn hearts towards God in Mark 3. Although Dietrich Bonhoeffer raged against the evil of Nazism, it was clear even to his executioners that his passion was for God's will and not his own. The medic who supervised his hanging later testified that *"In the almost fifty years that I worked as a doctor, I have hardly ever seen a man die so entirely submissive to the will of God."*[4]

So when Paul tells us in Ephesians 4:26 to *"Be angry and do not sin,"* he isn't simply warning us that anger can be sinful. He is telling us that not getting angry can be just as sinful too. He is telling us to stop gagging Jesus when he talks about anger. He is telling us to join with Jesus in righteous anger against the evil in the world.

---

3    He said this in an interview with the British *Daily Express* on 29th October 2008.

4    Quoted by Eberhard Bethge in *Dietrich Bonhoeffer: A Biography* (1967).

# 6

# Jesus on Sex

I lead a church which has a lot of young people. It doesn't really surprise me that they have one thing on their minds. I've lost count of the number of times that I've been asked where Jesus says that sex outside of marriage is wrong. When I try to answer, I know the follow-up question will be why on earth he says so.

Let me be clear. It isn't just people who don't want to follow Jesus who ask me those questions. Many of them are non-Christians who are processing the Gospel, and many others are newborn Christians who genuinely want to follow Christ. They are asking these questions in all seriousness, and I think that they deserve to be given a serious answer.

First things first. Let's note that Jesus doesn't actually talk much about sex before marriage. If he did, then we would begin to suspect that the text of the gospels had been tampered with, because first-century Jewish girls got married shortly after puberty. Since girls were usually married by the age of thirteen or fourteen, there wasn't much time for sex before marriage.[1] In a sex-saturated culture like ours it may be hard to imagine twelve- and thirteen-year-olds still acting like children and getting nervous rather than excited about their wedding night, but that's how it was in the first-century Jewish culture into which Jesus brought his teaching.

That said, adultery – sex *outside* marriage – was definitely an issue. The downside of parents marrying off their children young, often to relative strangers, was that not all first-century marriages were very happy. People were as predisposed as we are to want to have sex with other people's husbands and wives, albeit without some of the easy outlets which exist in our own culture to turn desire into action. This means we have to apply the three golden rules of understanding Scripture to Jesus' teaching about sex, by asking firstly *"What did Jesus say to his original hearers?"*, then asking secondly *"What is Jesus therefore saying to us today?"*, then asking thirdly *"How does Jesus want me to apply that teaching to my life?"* Let's apply these three rules to Matthew's account of some of Jesus' clearest teaching on sex and marriage:

> *Haven't you read... that at the beginning the Creator "made them male and female," and said "For this reason a man will leave his father and mother and be united to his wife, and the two will become one flesh"? So they are no longer two, but one flesh. Therefore what God has joined together, let no one separate.* (Matthew 19:4–6)

1    See Philip King and Lawrence Stager's book, *Life in Biblical Israel* (2001).

First, Jesus tells us that sex is very good! His teaching bears no resemblance to the Protestant male in the Monty Python movie *The Meaning of Life*, who boasts that he understands God's view of sex better than the Catholics while completely ignoring his wife's come-to-bed-with-me eyes. Nor does it resemble the negative teaching about sex which still dominates many of our churches, which Tony Campolo describes as *"Sex is a dirty, filthy thing, and you should save it for the person you marry"*![2]

Quite the contrary. Jesus draws our attention to the first two chapters of Genesis, where God creates humans male and female, tells them to go forth and multiply, and then declares that everything he has made (including the sex he has just encouraged) is *"very good"*. It was passages like this one, and the fact that the Old Testament book Song of Songs celebrates Solomon's sexual love for his young bride, which made Jesus' early followers write that *"the marriage bed should be **kept** pure"* and not *made* pure (Hebrews 13:4). If you haven't grasped that sex within marriage is one of God's greatest gifts to humans, then you have misunderstood Jesus' teaching.

Second, Jesus tells us that sex is better than good. It actually reflects something of the divine nature of God. He expects us to go back to the passage he quotes from and to read the whole of Genesis 1:26–27: *"God said, 'Let us make mankind in our image, in our likeness…' So God created mankind in his own image, in the image of God*

---

2    Tony Campolo in *Choose Love Not Power* (2009).

*he created them; male and female he created them."* Make sure you read those verses slowly. They tell us that God made humans male and female in order that we might reflect what he is like – *"in our image,"* as he puts it, referring to the three-in-one Trinity. For humankind, it's only two-in-one because we are not God, but it is two-in-one for a reason. Sex isn't merely recreational and consensual. It is an act of worship through which two human beings reflect the image of God – a God who is more than one person and yet One.

You've got to understand this as a central plank of Jesus' argument. It's why the Hebrew Law reserved the death penalty for very few offences compared to the other law codes of its day and yet included sexual sin among the handful of capital crimes. Jesus intervened to save an adulteress from being stoned to death in John 8, but he didn't play down the seriousness of her crime when he warned her to *"Go now and leave your life of sin."* The Old Testament treated sexual sin as a form of blasphemy, a vile parody of the Trinity, and Jesus endorsed and reinforced that view. Although he didn't talk much about sex *before* marriage because it wasn't much of an issue in his culture, we have already seen in the chapter on pornography and masturbation that he tightened up the Law when it came to adultery, declaring that even lusting after a person we are not married to puts us in danger of hellfire.

Third, and as a consequence of this, Jesus teaches us that sex does not belong to us but to God. That's pretty controversial in our culture, where anything goes sexually (and the painful consequences are everywhere), but it stands to reason when we grasp that God created us male and female and made sex one of the greatest human experiences in order to reflect his Triune glory to the world. We are like renters who have been allowed to live in an apartment which belongs to God, and God takes it very seriously when we start knocking down the walls of the apartment as if it actually belonged to us.

That's the bottom line when it comes to our following Jesus' words on sex. Jesus calls us to accept that our lives (sexual or otherwise) belong to God and not to ourselves. If we are willing to accept our Creator's boundaries, he tells us that sex is even better than we thought – not only can we enjoy it far better in its proper, God-created context, but we are also reflecting the glory of the Trinity when we do! But if we tell him that he can't be Lord of what we do in our bedrooms in private, we are fooling ourselves if we claim to be his followers in public.

Jesus hasn't finished. He still has one more big thing to say. He doesn't just talk about two becoming one, but starts talking about a person leaving his parents and being united to his wife (note the order) and then tells us that when such a public marriage covenant takes place it means that God has joined the two marriage partners together in a way which human laws alone cannot separate. The disciples don't know whether to be horrified that marriage is such a serious matter (they fear in verse 10 that it might be too holy a state to enter into at all), or to be overjoyed that God's plan for sex and marriage is so much better than they thought (we can tell from the New Testament letters that this second option ultimately won their hearts). Jesus tells us that we have only understood what he says about sex if we are similarly overawed and overjoyed.

This is what I try to explain to people when they ask what Jesus teaches about sex and why it seems so out of step with our Western culture. I explain what Jesus taught in these verses and throughout the rest of the gospels – that sex is reserved for our lifelong enjoyment within a marriage between one man and one woman, and that God created it to be so much fun so that we would have sex very often and enjoy it. I tell them that when a married couple make love they reflect the fact that God is like us, only infinitely greater. They are two-in-one, shining like the moon, while he is three-in-one, shining brighter than the sun.

If you are not living this way, sex should not be a reason for you to reject Jesus but a reason for you to accept him. Our culture is full of good reasons for bad sex, but Jesus promises that if we follow our Creator's instructions, sex will only get better. He also promises you forgiveness for your past sexual sins, as he did the adulterous woman in John 8:11, telling you that "*I do not condemn you; go now and leave your life of sin.*"

If you are not yet married but are trying to live Jesus' way, you should be encouraged. Jesus assures you that God prizes highly your decision not to have sex until you marry, and he promises that God will bless you as a result. Perhaps he is already planning your reward. Proverbs 18:22 tells us that *"He who finds a wife finds what is good and receives favour from the Lord."*

And if you are married, please don't focus more on Jesus' prohibitions on sex than you do on his great invitation. He encourages you to go and make love to your husband or wife to the glory of God! He tells you that some of your best worship should not be sung in church on a Sunday morning, but enjoyed in bed on a Sunday afternoon! In fact, shouldn't you stop reading this chapter and go forth to apply it for the glory of the Triune God?!

# 7

# JESUS ON DIVORCE AND REMARRIAGE

When Jesus taught his disciples in Matthew 19, they weren't just surprised by what he said about sex. They were also appalled by what he said about divorce and remarriage. Just like today, divorce was very common in the Roman Empire, so many Jewish rabbis had adapted their interpretation of the Old Testament to fit better with the changing times. John the Baptist had been one of the religious teachers who refused to do so, and King Herod had beheaded him for opposing his own marriage to a divorcee.[1] So when Jesus told the crowds how God feels about divorce and remarriage, his disciples were aghast. Matthew still remembers the incident vividly in his gospel:

---

1    Matthew 14:3–4. This is why the Pharisees "*came to Jesus to test him*". They hoped that his reply would provoke King Herod to execute him too.

*Some Pharisees came to Jesus to test him. They asked, "Is it lawful for a man to divorce his wife for any and every reason?" "Haven't you read," he replied, "that at the beginning the Creator 'made them male and female,' and said, 'For this reason a man will leave his father and mother and be united to his wife, and the two will become one flesh'? So they are no longer two, but one flesh. Therefore what God has joined together, let no one separate."*

*"Why then," they asked, "did Moses command that a man give his wife a certificate of divorce and send her away?" Jesus replied, "Moses permitted you to divorce your wives because your hearts were hard. But it was not this way from the beginning. I tell you that anyone who divorces his wife, except for sexual immorality, and marries another woman commits adultery."*

*The disciples said to him, "If this is the situation between a husband and wife, it is better not to marry."*
(Matthew 19:3–10)

Jesus' message is no more popular today than it was when he first spoke these words. If anything, the divorce rate in the Western world is even higher than it was in the Roman Empire. A third of the couples who married in 1995 are now divorced; half of those divorced couples have at least one child together; a third of those children never see one of their parents again. If you have experienced divorce first-hand – in your own marriage, in your parents' marriage, or in the marriages your friends – then you know something of the pain and devastation behind these numbers. We have grown so used to divorce as the open wound of our dysfunctional society that we find it a bit shocking that Jesus doesn't accept it as pragmatically as we do. We have grown so used to a domesticated Jesus that we find it surprising when he dares to challenge our own domestic issues.

Jesus debunks four common myths about divorce, and the first one is the idea that *divorce is normal*. Many first-century rabbis had taken a few words out of context in a verse in the Law of Moses – *"If a man marries a woman who becomes displeasing to him because he finds something indecent about her"* (Deuteronomy 24:1) – and had interpreted them to teach that divorce was permissible *"for any and every reason"*. The more liberal rabbis taught that *"something indecent"* included any form of incompatibility. If a woman burned her husband's dinner, put on weight or simply stopped looking as beautiful as the younger Jewish women, divorce was a valid option. That's why Matthew uses the Greek word *porneia*, which means *sexual immorality*, to make it clear that Jesus taught that *"something indecent"* meant discovering that she had been sexually unfaithful. Jesus redrew the line at which divorce was permissible, then he went on to teach why he had done so.

You may have noticed something peculiar about Jesus' reply to the Pharisees' question about divorce. They come to test him with a question about divorce, but he gives an answer which is far more focused on marriage. He points out that marriage was God's idea rather than our own, and that our Creator knew what he was doing. For all his mistakes, even the former British Prime Minister Tony Blair recognized that *"Strong families are the foundation of strong communities."*[2] Jesus says that they are all that and more. Marriages don't just reflect the three-in-one nature of God, but they also express the love relationship between Jesus and his Church (Ephesians 5:22–33). He therefore quotes from Genesis 2:24 to teach that God enables each married couple to unite, or literally *cleave together*, as one flesh. Divorce isn't normal. It is like a meat cleaver which slices through flesh which should never be divided. Divorce doesn't merely make a mockery of our wedding vows. It also blasphemes the nature and the loving character of the God before whom we made them.

Jesus' words must have pleased the conservatives, but he wasn't about to take sides. The second myth he debunks is the idea that *divorce is never allowed*. Conservatives tend to major on the fact that God says that he hates divorce in Malachi 2:16. What they forget is that he also describes himself as a divorcee in Isaiah 50:1 and Jeremiah 3:8. Jesus makes it clear that divorce *is* permitted in certain limited circumstances, because humans are so hardhearted that there are times when God will free a mistreated husband or wife from their marriage.[3] The example Jesus gives is of *porneia*, or *sexual immorality* through which one spouse

---

2    Tony Blair in his speech to the Labour Party Conference in Blackpool on 1st October 1996.

3    I know that things are rarely this black and white in a divorce, and that both parties often carry some of the blame. However, the fact that God is a completely innocent divorcee means that divorce itself is not a sin.

utterly betrays their marriage vows.[4] We can find two other examples elsewhere in the Bible. Exodus 21:10–11 suggests that serious and sustained abuse may be grounds for divorce – although it's usually best to allow impartial judges such as church leaders to determine whether this has actually happened. In 1 Corinthians 7:12–16 Paul suggests that if a spouse abandons the marital home and rejects every attempt at reconciliation over a long a period of time there may also be grounds for a divorce.

Jesus therefore infuriates liberals by saying that divorce is never normal, and that some level of incompatibility is simply part and parcel of marriage. He then infuriates conservatives by saying that divorce is not forbidden. He infuriates those who abuse, betray or abandon their spouse by saying that their spouse may be permitted to remarry but that they will not be.[5] When the disciples grasped that Jesus was teaching that anyone who causes the breakdown of their marriage is an adulterer if they remarry – even if the law of the land indulges their behaviour – they were so appalled that they exclaimed, *"If this is the situation between a husband and a wife, it is better not to marry."* You have not understood Jesus' teaching on divorce and remarriage unless it makes you want to exclaim something similar.

---

4    Since the normal Greek word for *adultery* is *moicheia*, some commentators argue that *porneia* has a broader meaning than just sex. However, Jesus is stopping us from using the "Bill Clinton argument" that certain types of sexual sin don't technically constitute adultery.

5    In case we try to explain away Matthew 19:9, Jesus repeats it in Matthew 5:32, Mark 10:11–12 and Luke 16:18.

You may be particularly interested in this chapter because you are in an unhappy marriage. If that's the case, you need to note that the third myth Jesus debunks is the idea that *divorce will solve the mess*. For those who feel trapped inside a loveless marriage, divorce can often feel like the answer. Those who embark on a trial separation tend to find themselves so elated by the taste of freedom that divorce quickly follows after. However, by reminding us that *"Moses permitted you to divorce your wives because your hearts were hard. But it was not this way from the beginning,"* Jesus emphasizes that divorce isn't the solution to the mess in our lives; it is part of the mess in our lives. It isn't even the preferred option if your partner has made divorce permissible for one of the three reasons I have listed in this chapter. God has made us a promise in Ezekiel 36:26 that he will turn our hard hearts into soft hearts if we let him. He is more passionate about helping your marriage to reflect the glories of his Triune nature and of Christ's love for the Church than even you are! If you are willing, then the entire might of heaven will rush towards you both to save and strengthen your rocky marriage.

In the meantime, as you seek to rebuild your marriage, God promises to come alongside you. He doesn't hate divorce because he wants to trap you in your marriage but because he has experienced the trauma of divorce first-hand. He knows the excruciating pain of divorce and that, without the healing effect of the Gospel, the wound never heals. He divorced unfaithful Israel but he didn't go looking for another wife. He waited patiently and wooed her back to restoration (Hosea 2:14–23). If your marriage is in a mess then God promises to help you, because so was his. He has the power to transform your broken marriage if you will let him.

The fourth and final myth Jesus debunks is that *divorce means your life is over*. Although he doesn't mention it specifically in this passage, when he talks of one flesh being hacked in two he drops a hint that there is hope for those who have been devastated by the trauma of divorce. When Jesus' body was broken on the cross, he cried out *"My God, my God, why have you abandoned me?"* (Matthew 27:46), because he bore all our pain in his body – not just our physical pain, but our emotional trauma too. When we treat divorce as the unforgivable sin, we forget what happened on the cross and we underestimate God's resurrection power. If you are divorced, Jesus probably doesn't have to convince you that it isn't normal and that it is excruciatingly painful, but he might need to convince you that his cross is greater than the sense of sin and guilt which so many divorcees feel. He might need to convince you that he will never reject you or abandon you, and that if you put your hand in his own nail-pierced hand then he will lead you on a journey to wholeness and happiness again.

Jesus tells us that marriage isn't just a convenience, a good excuse for a party, or a ticket to a tax break. It is a holy reflection of the Lord's covenant relationship with his People, and a proclamation of his marvellous Gospel. *"Therefore what God has joined together, let no one separate."*

# 8

# Jesus on Family

Jesus didn't have a public relations manager. It's probably just as well. If he had, then his PR manager would have been very disappointed when Jesus gave some teaching about family life. After offending the crowds through his teaching on stress, unforgiveness, possessions, pornography, masturbation, anger, sex, divorce and remarriage, this was surely a chance for him to say something which would make him a bit more popular. Nobody loved family life more than Jesus. He called God his Father, called his followers brothers and sisters, referred to himself as the Bridegroom, welcomed children to sit on his lap and loved his mother so much that his dying thoughts on the cross were to find her a new home (John 19:26–27). I can just imagine the look of disappointment on his PR manager's face when he heard what Jesus had to say:

*If anyone comes to me and does not hate father and mother, wife and children, brothers and sisters – yes,*

*even their own life – such a person cannot be my*
*disciple.* (Luke 14:26)

Jesus didn't have a PR manager, but it's easy to read
passages like this one and to think he ought to have had
one. It's very difficult to see why anyone would want to
crucify the gagged-and-bound Jesus, the dinner-party
Jesus, the invite-him-home-to-meet-your-parents
Jesus, but it's very easy to see why people wanted to
crucify this Jesus. We need to remember that it wasn't
the thieves or the drug dealers or the prostitutes who
killed Jesus. It was the respectable fathers of Israel who
preferred to murder God's Messiah than to accept his
constant challenge to their lifestyle.

I love children. I actually used to be one. For the
first sixteen years of my life all of my best friends were
children, and now I have four children of my own. I
am the kind of person that, if I were to die, would be
described at my funeral as "a devoted family man".
That's why I need to listen carefully to what Jesus says
about families. He warns that children are often the major
idols which are worshipped in respectable homes.

I live in a residential part of London which is full of
yummy mummies and devoted dads who build their
lives around their children. It would be safer to come
between a she-bear and her cubs than to challenge
the people in my neighbourhood about their child-
centred lives. Yet Jesus didn't just know how to accept
rejection; he also knew how to reject acceptance. He
went after respectable parents – the people most likely
to be found in Western churches on a Sunday – and he

launched a full-frontal attack on the most cherished idols in their lives.

We tend not to be as offended by verses like this one as we ought to be. We simply shrug off Jesus' call to hate our children and parents and siblings as a piece of preacher's hyperbole. Even if somebody points out that *miseō* is a very strong Greek word which doesn't just mean *to hate* but *to detest* or *to pursue with hatred*, we don't get overly concerned. We gag Jesus and simply misinterpret his message as *don't love your family as much as you love me.* The problem is that this verse is part of a larger passage which shows us that Jesus isn't talking about loving our families less but about dying to their love and approval. He continues:

> *Whoever does not carry their cross and follow me cannot be my disciple.*
>
> *Suppose one of you wants to build a tower. Won't you first sit down and estimate the cost to see if you have enough money to complete it? For if you lay the foundation and are not able to finish it, everyone who sees it will ridicule you, saying, "This person began to build and wasn't able to finish."*
>
> *Or suppose a king is about to go to war against another king. Won't he first sit down and consider whether he is able with ten thousand men to oppose the one coming against him with twenty thousand? If he is not able, he will send a delegation while the other is still a long way off and will ask for terms of peace. In the same way, those of you who do not give up everything you have cannot be my disciples.* (Luke 14:27–33)

If you or I were to talk about carrying a cross, we might be guilty of using preacher's hyperbole. Not Jesus. He gave this teaching on the back of several predictions that his enemies were about to crucify him in order to silence his words.[1] He explains in verse 26 what he means by hating the members of our own family by telling us in verse 27 that following him means dying to all that we hold dearest in our lives, including our loved ones – *especially* our loved ones. Let me illustrate by telling you about what these verses have meant practically for three of my friends.

When the Lord used a miracle to capture the attention of my next-door neighbour Gaynor, my wife and I were able to invite her to our church. She experienced a second miracle while she was listening to the sermon, when the Lord gave her a supernatural vision which resulted in her conversion. When she got home and told her husband, however, he made it clear that she couldn't have two men in her life. She had to choose between Jesus and him. He threatened to divorce her if she ever went back to church or ever spoke to him about her new-found faith again. Gaynor discovered that Jesus gave this teaching for a reason. Real faith makes real waves which create real enemies and which force us to make real choices.

When my friend Hannah heard the Gospel, she was converted. As a sixteen-year-old Pakistani Muslim in the north of England, she wasn't ready for the venom which was unleashed when she told her father and her brothers. She still cries when she talks about the

1    Luke 9:22–23, 44; 13:31–33.

day her father led a mob of Muslim friends into the house to kill her and she escaped death by hiding in a cupboard in the bathroom. Jesus knew that his teaching wouldn't please a PR manager. He said these things because he wanted to prepare us for the difficult and very costly choices which always accompany genuine Christian conversion.

When my friend Paul heard the Gospel, he was converted. He knew enough about Jesus' teaching on sex to grasp that this meant that his gay lifestyle needed to change. He didn't know at the time that God would lead him on a path which would cause him to fall in love with a beautiful woman and raise a family of boys. He only knew that following Jesus felt like being crucified every single day. He knew why men need to check their budget before building a tower, why kings need to count their armies before marching into battle, and why people – homosexual or heterosexual – need to count the cost before surrendering their lives to Jesus.

In some ways, people like Gaynor and Hannah and Paul are much more fortunate than many other Western Christians. For single people, conversion presents new opportunities to meet a marriage partner. For parents, it offers a safe environment in which to raise a family. Following Jesus can sound like a series of upsides. Muslims and homosexuals normally understand much more clearly from the outset that there is a reason why Jesus described Christian conversion as dying. Gaynor had to choose between Jesus and her husband (he was bluffing, by the way). Hannah had to choose between Jesus and her entire family. Paul had to choose between Jesus and his gay lifestyle. So it shouldn't surprise us that we need to surrender our own family relationships to Jesus too. It isn't a question of *whether* following Jesus will cost us everything. It is simply a question of *what* and *when*.

I was on the receiving end of Jesus' teaching when I told my parents I had no interest in going to church with them as a teenager. I hated the fact that my dad refused to listen to my protests and told me I would have to go to church with the family until I was eighteen. I resented him for not listening to his well-meaning friends who tried to warn him that forcing me to go to church would only cause me to resent the Christian faith when I was older. I wasn't converted until after I left home, but I know it was as a direct result of his evident commitment to do what he felt was right as a Christian parent, even when he saw that it made me very angry and resentful.

My wife and children were on the receiving end of Jesus' teaching when I sensed a call from God to relocate to London in order to pastor the group of believers who would go on to become Everyday Church. I don't know why God chose such an inconvenient moment in our lives to confront us with their invitation – only two or three days after the birth of my baby daughter – but I do know that my wife was still recovering from childbirth and spent a lot of time in tears. When she sensed God's call herself and helped me to break the news to our sons, we discovered that it is even more painful to watch those we love suffer because of our decisions than it is to suffer ourselves. As I drove my eldest son from his last day at school to our new home in London, he asked with all the naivety of a child, *"Daddy, when everyone in London has started following Jesus can we move back here so that I can go to school with all my friends?"* I covered my face so that he wouldn't see the tears in my eyes and reminded myself that a father's job is not to make his children happy in the short-term, but to teach them how to surrender everything to God.[2]

I also had to remind myself that the Gospel is the message that a Father gave up his only Son to save us from our sin (John 3:16). It is the message that a Son was willing to be abandoned by his Father so that we could become part of his heavenly family (Mark 15:34). It is a call to follow the one who distanced himself from his mother and his brothers so that we could be brought near to God (Matthew 12:46–50).

Families may be very respectable idols, but Jesus tells us they are often idols all the same. Let's not allow our families to stop us from taking up our crosses daily and living for the one who took up his cross so that we might live at all.

---

2    God says this to parents in passages such as Deuteronomy 6:1–7 and Proverbs 22:6.

# 9

# JESUS ON POVERTY

Jesus told many much loved parables. The Parable of
the Sheep and the Goats, however, isn't one of them.
Even unbelievers tend to praise the beauty of Jesus'
parables, but I haven't met any who praise this parable
about poverty. It is Jesus at his most offensive:

> *When the Son of Man comes in his glory, and all the*
> *angels with him, he will sit on his glorious throne. All*
> *the nations will be gathered before him, and he will*
> *separate the people one from another as a shepherd*
> *separates the sheep from the goats. He will put the*
> *sheep on his right and the goats on his left.*
>
> *Then the King will say to those on his right,*
> *"Come, you who are blessed by my Father; take your*
> *inheritance, the kingdom prepared for you since the*
> *creation of the world. For I was hungry and you gave*
> *me something to eat, I was thirsty and you gave me*
> *something to drink, I was a stranger and you invited*
> *me in, I needed clothes and you clothed me, I was sick*

*and you looked after me, I was in prison and you came
to visit me."*

*Then the righteous will answer him, "Lord, when
did we see you hungry and feed you, or thirsty and
give you something to drink? When did we see you
a stranger and invite you in, or needing clothes and
clothe you? When did we see you sick or in prison and
go to visit you?" The King will reply, "Truly I tell you,
whatever you did for one of the least of these brothers
and sisters of mine, you did for me."*

*Then he will say to those on his left, "Depart from
me, you who are cursed, into the eternal fire prepared
for the devil and his angels. For I was hungry and you
gave me nothing to eat, I was thirsty and you gave
me nothing to drink, I was a stranger and you did not
invite me in, I needed clothes and you did not clothe me,
I was sick and in prison and you did not look after me."*

*They also will answer, "Lord, when did we see you
hungry or thirsty or a stranger or needing clothes or
sick or in prison, and did not help you?" He will reply,
"Truly I tell you, whatever you did not do for one of the
least of these, you did not do for me."*

*Then they will go away to eternal punishment, but
the righteous to eternal life.* (Matthew 25:31–46)

Many people get offended by Jesus' teaching about
hell in this parable. Hold that thought because that
will be the topic of the next chapter. Other people get
offended that Jesus appears to be teaching that we can
get to heaven by our own good deeds. That's easier
to answer because the context of the parable makes

it clear that Jesus isn't teaching salvation by works at all. He confronts false believers with their hypocrisy in chapter 23, promises to judge them in chapter 24 and gives a series of illustrations in chapter 25 which warn that God will judge those who say they honour him but follow a Messiah of their own making. Jesus warns that they will be seen for what they are by their unreadiness (25:1–13) and by the laziness of their devotion to God (25:14–30). This parable is therefore a warning that how we treat the poor is a mark of whether we are truly following Jesus at all.[1]

In case you haven't noticed, capitalism is in crisis. The gulf between rich and poor nations is getting bigger, and so is the gulf between the rich and poor within each nation. It's not hard to poke holes in the theology of the anti-capitalist protesters who chained themselves to the pulpit of St Paul's Cathedral in London in October 2012, shouting that *"In the fight for economic justice, Jesus threw the money changers out of the temple, but you invited them in and instead evicted us,"*[2] but it is also hard to pretend that they haven't got a serious point. For centuries the Western church has allied itself with feudal landlords, with oppressive rulers and with money interests instead of with the poor. We need to take Jesus very seriously when he warns us that how we treat the poor shows what we think of him, and that what we think of him shows whether we are truly saved at all.

---

1    It directly parallels Ezekiel 34 which also says that those who oppress the poor are not God's People at all.

2    Reported in *The Guardian* newspaper on 14th October 2012.

Jesus tells us in this parable that *how we treat the poor reveals what we truly think of him*. In the classic 1980s movie *Coming to America*, Eddie Murphy plays a rich African prince who cannot find true love. Every woman in the world wants to marry him because of his money, so he flies to New York and disguises himself as a pauper in order to find out what people truly feel towards him rather than towards what he can do for them. The Bible says that Jesus does the same thing by coming to us through people who are in need. "*I was hungry... I was thirsty... I was a stranger... I needed clothes... I was sick... I was in prison,*" he challenges us. Yes, it's true that the reference to "*brothers and sisters*" means that he is specifically referring to the poor within the Church, but let's not use that to squirm out of his general challenge.[3] Jesus perceives our heart towards him by how we treat those who are in need around us. He hates it when we have one face for him on Sunday and another for the poor and needy from Monday to Saturday.

Jesus also tells us in this parable that *how we treat the poor reveals what we truly think of the Gospel.* There are plenty of fine-sounding reasons we can give for not helping the poor, but those who have truly responded to the Gospel know that Jesus could have used every single one of them not to save us. We say, "The poor don't deserve our help because they have brought their poverty on themselves," but Jesus could have just as easily said the same of us. The essence of

3    Proverbs 19:17 and Acts 22:7–8 also tell us that the Lord comes to us through believers in need.

the Gospel is that the holy Son of God shed his blood for the guilty and undeserving! We say, "The poor are likely to abuse my kindness," but Jesus might have said the same thing about us and with far greater reason. We complain that "It's my money!" but Jesus might have said the same about his blood. John 3:16 tells us that the Gospel is the news that *"God so loved the world that he gave his one and only Son, that whoever believes in him shall not perish but have eternal life,"* and 1 John 3:16 tells us how to respond to this Gospel: *"Jesus Christ laid down his life for us. And we ought to lay down our lives for our brothers and sisters."*

Genuine Christians have always understood this. While the Romans tended to despise the poor and to view their misery as largely self-inflicted, the early Christians won the Empire to Christ by demonstrating the Gospel by the way they helped the poor. The last pagan emperor, Julian the Apostate, was forced to complain to one of his priests that *"It is disgraceful that… while the impious Galileans support both their own poor and ours as well, everyone sees that our people lack aid from us!"*[4]

The Church has always been this unstoppable whenever she has demonstrated the Gospel by loving the poor. The last great revival in Europe and America was led by William Booth and The Salvation Army, so we need to note the reason given by his biographers for why his revival advanced so powerfully: *"His principal message was the importance of not attempting –*

---

4    Emperor Julian wrote this in 362 AD in a letter to Arsacius, the pagan high priest of Galatia.

*before the remedy was applied – to distinguish between the deserving and the undeserving poor."*[5]

Jesus also tells us in this parable that *how we treat the poor reveals what we truly think of the age to come.* It is interesting that the "goats" in this parable clearly view themselves as believers. They call Jesus *"Lord"* and they appear very willing to help him in theory. Unfortunately for them, Jesus does not judge people based on their intentions but based on their deeds. If we love our money too much to give it away then we prove that, however much we protest to the contrary, we are still children of this age. We haven't truly been transformed by the grace which caused Zacchaeus to give his money to the poor (Luke 19:1–10), which caused the early Christians to sell their fields after Pentecost to help the poor (Acts 2:44–45 and 4:34–35), which caused Francis of Assisi to strip off in the courtroom and which caused Charles T. Studd to turn his back on fame and fortune to live among the poor of inland China.

If you live in America or Europe and you earn an average salary, you are roughly the 57-millionth richest person in the world. If you earn more than the average salary, you are even higher up the global rich list. I know that our cost of living is higher than in other parts of the world, but I still have to take it seriously when a recent UNICEF report tells me that the amount of money I spent on taking my wife to the cinema last week could have fed a starving child for a

5    Roy Hattersley in *Blood and Fire: William and Catherine Booth and Their Salvation Army* (1999).

month on the other side of the world. Jesus warns us in this parable that what we think of him and his Gospel and his promises about the age to come is not proven by what we say, but by what we do. If we truly believe that Jesus shed his blood for us (all of it and not just 5 or 10 per cent of it), we will show it through the way we give to those who are in need. We will view them as Jesus in disguise and will live in such a way that he can tell us when he returns that *"Whatever you did for one of the least of these brothers and sisters of mine, you did for me."*

John Wesley, the leader of another revival which showed that the rapid advance of the Gospel is inextricably linked to its demonstration through our deep love for the poor, told his friends that *"If I leave behind me ten pounds, you and all mankind bear witness against me that I lived and died a thief and a robber."* Sure enough, he gave away so much of his large income that when he died his estate consisted merely of one coat and two teaspoons.[6] He echoes Jesus' teaching in the Parable of the Sheep and the Goats when he warns us that anyone who hangs onto anything more than *"the plain necessaries of life – not delicacies, not superfluities... lives in an open, habitual denial of the Lord... You have thrown away the treasure in heaven: God and Christ are lost. You have gained riches, and hell-fire."*[7]

---

6    Wesley writing in 1744, quoted by J. Wesley Bready in *England Before and After Wesley* (1938).

7    He preached this in 1748, preserved by Albert Outler in *John Wesley's Sermons: An Anthology* (1991).

# 10

## JESUS ON HELL

The English philosopher Bertrand Russell hated Jesus and he wasn't afraid to say so. He explained why he hated him in his bestselling book *Why I Am Not a Christian*:

> *There is one very serious defect to my mind in Christ's moral character, and that is that He believed in hell. I do not myself feel that any person who is really profoundly humane can believe in everlasting punishment. Christ certainly as depicted in the Gospels did believe in everlasting punishment... I really do not think that a person with a proper degree of kindliness in his nature would have put fears and terrors of that sort into the world...*
>
> *Remember about the sheep and the goats; how at the second coming He is going to divide the sheep from the goats, and He is going to say to the goats: "Depart from me, ye cursed, into everlasting fire." He continues, "And these shall go away into everlasting fire"... I must say that I think all this doctrine, that hell-fire is*

*a punishment for sin, is a doctrine of cruelty. It is a doctrine that put cruelty into the world and gave the world generations of cruel torture; and the Christ of the Gospels, if you could take Him as His chroniclers represent Him, would certainly have to be considered partly responsible for that.*[1]

We saw in the previous chapter that many people would like to gag Jesus to stop him from telling the Parable of the Sheep and the Goats because they don't like his teaching on poverty. Even those who would like to enlist him as a spokesman for their charitable causes tend to avoid that parable because they are so offended by its teaching on hell. Many Christians confess that this is an area where they feel most embarrassed by Jesus' teaching and are most tempted to gag him. C.S. Lewis admitted that "There is no doctrine which I would more willingly remove from Christianity than this, if it lay in my power. But it has the full support of Scripture and, specially, of Our Lord's own words."[2] More recently, the bestselling Christian author Rob Bell has questioned whether Jesus really said what Bertrand Russell complained about at all:

*"God wants all people to be saved and to come to a knowledge of the truth" (1 Timothy 2). So does God get what God wants? How great is God? Great enough to achieve what God sets out to do, or kind of great, medium great, great most of the time, but in this, the fate of billions of people, not totally great. Sort of great.*

1    Bertrand Russell in his essay *Why I Am Not a Christian* (1927).
2    C.S. Lewis in *The Problem of Pain* (1940).

*A little great… History is not tragic, hell is not forever, and love, in the end, wins.*[3]

Jesus talked about hell more than the whole of the Old Testament combined, so we have to ask ourselves why Jesus decided to offend us by talking so clearly and consistently about hell. We have to discover whether we are at liberty to tone down his language as Rob Bell suggests, or whether he talked so much about hell because it matters so much to us all. Let's draw out five reasons this parable gives us why Jesus taught so offensively about hell.

First, Jesus talked a lot about hell because *he wants us to grasp that it is real.* Rob Bell quotes from the third-century works of Origen to argue that Christians have not always interpreted Jesus' teaching on hell in the same way, but he fails to mention that the Second Church Council of Constantinople declared that Origen and anyone else who tried to water down his teaching was either disingenuous or deluded. It seems odd to me that, while bishops and church leaders and Christian writers often struggle to understand what Jesus means, non-Christians do not seem to share their problem. The atheist philosopher Ray Bradley laughs at the way that Christians seek to gag Jesus on this issue, pointing out that this *"would be to suppose that Jesus was either mistaken or misreported. But if Jesus was mistaken, he can't be divine. And if Jesus was misreported, then the Bible can't be the true Word of God. A believer has no option, then, but to accept the doctrine of hellfire."*[4]

---

3    Rob Bell in *Love Wins* (2011).
4    Professor Ray Bradley of Simon Fraser University in Vancouver,

Second, Jesus talked a lot about hell because *he wants us to grasp how terrible it is*. He explains in this parable that hell is *"the eternal fire prepared for the devil and his angels"* – in other words, it is a place which he personally created to be the place of punishment for Satan and his demons. He doesn't want any of us to be deceived into joining them there because we think that hell simply means nothingness, so he deliberately parallels "eternal punishment" and "eternal life" in this parable. Augustine of Hippo, one of the greatest theologians in the history of the Church, noted that *"The phrases are parallel: eternal punishment and eternal life. To say in the same context, 'Eternal life will be endless but eternal punishment will have an end' is utterly ridiculous. Since the eternal life of the saints will be endless, the eternal punishment of those who incur it will surely be endless."*[5] "Fire" may indeed be a metaphor, like "sheep" and "goats", but if that's the case then it is a metaphor for something unspeakably painful. The eighteenth-century theologian Jonathan Edwards observed that *"When metaphors are used in Scripture about spiritual things... they fall short of the literal truth."*[6] Jesus uses metaphors to describe a hell which is far more terrible than we can imagine.

Third, Jesus talked a lot about hell because *he wants us to grasp that our actions in this life have eternal*

---

Canada, made this observation during a formal debate in 1994 with William L. Craig over the question "Can a Loving God Send People to Hell?"

5    Augustine writing in 426 AD in his seminal work *The City of God* (21.23).

6    Taken from his sermon "The Torments of Hell Are Exceedingly Great" in *Sermons and Discourses 1723–29*.

*consequence*. Rob Bell is right that God gets what he wants, but Jesus tells us that what he wants is a human race which chooses either to love him or reject him. He won't force himself upon us like a rapist. He woos us and he warns us that our response to him will echo through eternity. Ben Witherington, a professor in New Testament studies and a frequent guest on The History Channel and The Discovery Channel, explains that

> *Hell in the New Testament is a constant reminder that there is a final accountability for our beliefs and behaviours in this life, whatever the particulars and temperature and durability of Hell may be. It is a reminder that this life is basically the time of decision, and the decisions we make now can indeed have eternal consequences in the afterlife. And, frankly, this is not bad news. It is a part of the Good News that in the end justice as well as mercy, righteousness as well as compassion, and holiness as well as love wins.[7]*

Fourth, Jesus talked a lot about hell because *he wants to encourage us that God is just and fair*. We tend to cast ourselves as either sheep or goats in this parable and therefore complain about hell, but we need to remember that many people in history have been the victims of injustice whose cause Jesus champions at this Final Judgment. When Pol Pot died in 1998, having never been brought to justice for murdering 1.5 million Cambodians during his four years of rule, *The Sun* newspaper published a cartoon of him in torment

---

7    He wrote this in a blog on the interfaith website *Patheos* on 16th March 2011.

underneath a caption which read, *"We hope that Pol Pot is burning in Hell"*. When even a British newspaper, which is famous for its topless Page Three Girls, starts crying out for a God of justice, it should make us think twice about gagging Jesus for his teaching about hell. It was ironic that in the same week that *Time* magazine focused on Rob Bell's book with a front cover which asked *"What if there's no hell?"* the New York *Daily News* reported the killing of Osama Bin Laden with its own front page which shouted in even bigger letters, *"Rot in Hell!"* Jesus talked so much about hell because to victims of injustice and wickedness it is actually very good news. The word "Hallelujah" occurs only four times in the New Testament and all of them are in Revelation 19:1–10 when God reveals that he will ensure that justice is done forever.

Fifth, Jesus therefore talked a lot about hell because *he wants to warn us that we all need a Saviour*. Few people complain that God should send the architects of genocide and terrorist atrocities to hell. We complain that he should send people like us there, but that is precisely what Jesus wants us to understand and fear. The goats in the parable are not people who have committed terrible crimes but simply those who have not done the good that God called them to do. Jesus told this parable in order to emphasize that even the best human beings are not good enough for heaven. He tells us that each of our earthly sins requires eternal punishment because they are sins against the eternal and infinite God – as John Piper reminds us: *"Degrees* *of blameworthiness come not from how **long** you offend dignity, but from **how high** the dignity is that you offend.*"[8] Hell is no more of an overreaction to sin on God's part than the sacrificial death of his only Son on the cross so that we don't need to go there. Jesus described the horrors of hell because he was about to endure them in our place and because he doesn't want us to fool ourselves that his sacrifice is an optional extra for people less respectable than ourselves.

None of this means that Jesus' teaching on hell is less offensive. It just helps us to understand why we need to let it offend us and change us. It shows us why it is foolish to complain with Bertrand Russell and Rob Bell that hell sounds horrible. It shows why hell is just and necessary and fair, and it even shows us why God's People see hell as a reason to praise the Lord for his commitment to punish every act of wrongdoing in Revelation 19:1–10. How we react to Jesus' teaching on hell doesn't say as much about him as it does about ourselves. It reveals whether we are sheep or goats. It reveals whether we have laid hold of God's salvation for ourselves.

*"Do I take any pleasure in the death of the wicked?"* the Lord asks in Ezekiel 18. *"Rather, am I not pleased when they turn from their ways and live?... For I take no pleasure in the death of anyone, declares the Sovereign Lord. Repent and live!"*

---

8    John Piper in *Let the Nations Be Glad* (1993).

# 11

# JESUS ON HIMSELF

So far we have focused on what Jesus said about *issues*. We have seen that many people want to gag him because of his teaching on issues such as money and pornography and sex and divorce and hell. But although these issues got him hated, we mustn't miss the fact that Jesus wasn't crucified for what he said about issues. He was crucified for what he taught about *himself*.

Jesus claimed that he was God. That's so obvious from the gospel accounts that we need to gag him on virtually every page if we want to deny it. He came into a Jewish culture in which the idea of God coming down to earth in human flesh was scandalous, and yet he taught in such a way that Peter exclaimed, *"You are the Messiah, the Son of the Living God"* (Matthew 16:16). Even his most cynical disciple, Thomas, learned to worship him as *"My Lord and my God!"* (John 20:28). Even his Roman executioners exclaimed in horror at the foot of the cross that "*Surely he was the Son of God!*" (Matthew 27:54).

It's interesting that Jesus' enemies did not try to deny that he claimed to be God. In fact, it was the reason they sought to kill him. They started plotting when they heard him "*calling God his own Father, making himself equal with God*" (John 5:18). They argued furiously among themselves, "*Who is this fellow who speaks blasphemy? Who can forgive sins but God alone?*" (Luke 5:21). They accused him of "*blasphemy, because you, a mere man, claim to be God*" (John 10:33), and they ultimately made this the grounds for his execution (Mark 14:64). Whatever else we might say about Jesus' enemies, they at least had one thing going for them: they understood perfectly that he was claiming to be Yahweh, the God of Israel, come down to earth in human flesh.

People who want to gag Jesus and to use him as their ventriloquist's dummy get very uncomfortable with the idea that he is God. It is one thing to hijack a human teacher and enlist him as a spokesman for their cause, but no one really wants to try and kidnap the Living God. It would be safer to jump into the big cats' enclosure at the zoo and to try and kidnap a tiger. That's why people have always looked for reasons to gag Jesus when he talks about himself. They know that if the carpenter from Nazareth is truly God then everything about the way we live our lives has to change.

Some people opt to believe in the *non-historical Jesus*. That's probably one of the reasons why Dan

Brown's novel *The Da Vinci Code* sold over 100 million copies. I have lost count of the number of people I have talked to who found it in the fiction section of their local bookstore and yet who truly believe the novel's fundamental assertion: *"Almost everything our fathers taught us about Christ is **false**... Jesus was viewed by His followers as a mortal prophet... a great and powerful man, but a **man** nonetheless... Jesus' establishment as 'the Son of God' was officially proposed and voted on by the Council of Nicaea... a relatively close vote at that."*[1] You only have to go to the travel section of the same bookstore to discover that Dan Brown's Jesus isn't Jesus at all. *The Rough Guide to the Da Vinci Code* observes that *"There is a cheerful sloppiness about the way Dan Brown strings together people, places, incidents and ideas... It is a mishmash of historical nonsense... Dan Brown is effectively saying that the institution of the Church is built on a lie. But the lie is Dan Brown's and it is deliberate."*[2]

Other people opt to believe in *Jesus the good teacher*. They say kind things about his parables, but when the rubber hits the road they treat his teaching as a collection of pithy thoughts, motivational speeches and fortune-cookie wisdom. They pick and choose between his sayings and they don't stop to listen to the way he rebuked the rich young ruler in Mark 10. When the man tried to flatter him by addressing him as *"Good teacher"*, Jesus corrected him by asking, *"Why do you call me good? No one is good – except God alone."*

1    Dan Brown in *The Da Vinci Code* (2003).

2    Michael and Veronica Haag, *The Rough Guide to the Da Vinci Code* (2004).

He refused to allow the rich young ruler to treat him as nothing more than a good teacher. He is either God or he is a lousy teacher, since the bedrock of his teaching was the claim that he is God.

Other people opt to believe in *Jesus the prophet*. One of my close friends is a Muslim who likes to point out that Jesus is the most mentioned prophet in the Qur'an, but when I ask him what he prophesied he starts to get uncomfortable. The only reason he can continue in his belief that Jesus was nothing more than a prophet is that the imam of his mosque has forbidden him from reading any of the gospels. Jesus refuses to be gagged in this matter, so our only option if we choose not to believe it is to bury our heads in the sand.[3]

C.S. Lewis, the author of *The Chronicles of Narnia*, was converted to Christ through a discussion with J.R.R. Tolkien, the author of *The Lord of the Rings*. He explained later that his conversion was due to examining afresh what Jesus actually taught about himself:

> *I am trying to prevent anyone saying the really foolish thing that people often say about Him: "I'm ready to accept Jesus as a great moral teacher, but I don't accept His claim to be God." That is the one thing we must not say. A man who was merely a man and said the sort of things Jesus said would not be a great moral teacher. He would either be a lunatic – on a level with the man who says he is a poached egg – or he would be*

---

3    In Luke 24:19 and 25, Jesus specifically rebukes people for thinking he is merely a prophet. He exclaims, *"How foolish you are, and how slow to believe!"*

*the Devil of Hell. You must make your choice. Either this man was, and is, the Son of God: or else a madman or something worse. You can shut Him up for a fool, you can spit at Him and kill Him as a demon; or you can fall at His feet and call Him Lord and God. But let us not come with any patronising nonsense about His being a great human teacher. He has not left that open to us. He did not intend to.[4]*

C.S. Lewis is right. We need to make a choice. And after ten chapters about Jesus' teaching we are in a position to do so. We have already touched on five areas of proof which should convince us that Jesus is exactly who he says he is. We need to take these proofs seriously, because Jesus is asking us to make a choice to gag him or to glorify him.

First, there is *Jesus' teaching*. It hasn't just been revered by people in the West. It has been recognized as divinely inspired all around the world. Mahatma Gandhi was a Hindu but described him as *"One of the greatest teachers humanity has ever had."*[5] It begs the question: Are these the teachings of a madman or imposter who lied that he was God, or are they held in such high universal regard because they truly are the oracles of God?

Second, there is *Jesus' character*. Claiming to be God isn't easy, especially if your life is subjected to non-stop scrutiny for three years by your enemies and your friends. Since God never sins, it requires only one

---

4    C.S. Lewis in *Mere Christianity* (1952).
5    Gandhi said this in *The Modern Review* in October 1941.

moment of weakness to prove that a person is not God. Follow me around for three hours and you will see this quite clearly, but people followed Jesus for three years and still concluded that he had never done anything wrong. Nobody followed him more closely than Peter, who testified that *"He committed no sin, and no deceit was found in his mouth"* (1 Peter 2:22). Nobody wanted to prove that Jesus had sinned more than the Jewish priests, yet they could only sentence him to death for his claim to be God and not for any other charge which they could level against him (Matthew 26:59–66).

Third, there are *Jesus' miracles*. It's important to note that Jesus' early enemies did not attempt to deny that he turned water into wine, healed lepers, walked on water, raised the dead and fed 5,000 with five loaves and two small fish. All they could argue was that Jesus performed these miracles because he was an expert in black magic.[6] Two centuries later, Christians still pointed out that their enemies, *"unable to resist the miracles which Jesus is recorded to have performed, speak of them slanderously as works of sorcery."*[7]

Fourth, there is *Jesus' resurrection*. We haven't space to look at it in much detail here,[8] but it is one of the greatest proofs that Jesus is God. The Oxford professor Géza Vermes published his analysis of the

---

6    For example in Matthew 9:34, 10:25 and 12:22–32. This led to Peter's statement in Acts 2:22.

7    Origen pointed this out in about 248 AD in *Contra Celsum* (chapter 48).

8    If you want more details, I examine the facts behind the resurrection of Jesus much more fully in my in-depth study of one of the gospels, entitled *Straight to the Heart of Matthew* (2010).

views that someone stole Jesus' body or went to the wrong tomb or simply made up the entire story, and he concludes that

> *When every argument has been considered and weighed, the only conclusion acceptable to the historian must be that the opinions of the orthodox, the liberal sympathiser and the critical agnostic alike – and even perhaps of the disciples themselves – are simply interpretations of the one disconcerting fact: namely that the women who set out to pay their last respects to Jesus found to their consternation, not a body, but an empty tomb.[9]*

Fifth and finally, there is the existence of the Church. When Jesus was crucified, his 120 faithful followers abandoned him, hid behind locked doors and acted as if the Christian dream were over. A few days later they reappeared, convinced that they had seen the risen Jesus and willing to die rather than deny it. The Cambridge professor C.F.D. Moule points out that the growth and triumph of the Church from this handful of Galilean peasants "rips a great hole in history, a hole the size and shape of the resurrection… What does the secular historian propose to stop it up with?"[10]

Jesus claimed to be God. He gave five proofs that it is true. Now each of us has to decide. Will we listen to who he says he is or will we dare to try and gag the Living God?

9    Géza Vermes in his book *Jesus the Jew: A Historian's Reading of the Gospels* (1973).
10   C.F.D. Moule in *The Phenomenon of the New Testament* (1967).

# 12

# JESUS ON DIFFERENT RELIGIONS

I was really excited when I got Siri on my iPhone. If you aren't an iPhone user, let me explain. Siri enables you to speak questions into your phone and hear your phone speak back an answer. One of the first questions I asked was *"What is the meaning of life?"* and Siri sidestepped the question by telling me, *"It is a film by Monty Python."* Undeterred, I repeated the question and got a different answer: *"Try to be nice to people, avoid eating fat, read a good book every now and then, get some walking in, and try to live together in peace and harmony with people of all creeds and nations."* That left me with a question which even Siri cannot answer. If even my phone knows how to behave itself in a multi-faith society, then why is Jesus so offensive when he talks about different religions?

Jesus didn't need an iPhone to know that people would consider him arrogant for his teaching in John

**14:6:** *"I am the way and the truth and the life. No one comes to the Father except through me."* He knew that the Jews would be offended by his charge that their meticulous obedience to Moses' Law could never save them, and he knew that the Romans would be offended by his charge that their plethora of gods and goddesses were nothing more than lifeless idols. He knew that people in multi-faith societies like ours would see his teaching as the breaking of the ultimate taboo. He knew that making an exclusive claim that there is only one Saviour is seen as excruciatingly offensive and arrogant in a multi-faith society. But he refuses to let us gag him because he wants to expose the hidden arrogance which lurks beneath the tolerant veneer of our own Western worldview.

Jesus exposes the Western worldview as arrogant *because it denies the reality of sin.* Although it pretends to embrace all the great religions of the world, it actually denies the central teaching which lies at the heart of all of them. It isn't just Christians, Jews and Muslims who talk about sin and Final Judgment. Hindus, Buddhists, Jains and Sikhs also teach that evil deeds create bad karma. There has never been a culture in human history – not even in secular Europe – which denies that bad deeds incur some kind of spiritual guilt and punishment. When Westerners act as if God will forgive them for their sin, regardless of their religion or their lack of it, they aren't being humble. They are drowning out the sound of their own consciences and assuming that they know better than the religious teachings of every people group in every part of the world in every generation. It couldn't be more arrogant.

Jesus exposes the Western worldview as arrogant *because it denies that sin must be atoned for through sacrifice*. He isn't claiming that every religion except for Christianity is entirely wrong. He is affirming that the great world religions are basically right when they teach that sinners will be punished unless they offer God an atoning sacrifice. Most Westerners are as lazy as Homer Simpson when he screams in the face of death, *"I'm gonna die! Jesus, Allah, Buddha – I love you all!"*[1] We haven't had the humility to study the world religions enough to grasp that forgiveness for sin always requires a sacrifice.

The Ancient Greeks taught that Hercules needed to perform twelve labours in order to appease the gods for murdering his family. They taught that King Agamemnon needed to sacrifice his daughter in order to appease the gods before they would bless him in his war against Troy. An ancient Sanskrit epic teaches Hindus that King Ravana amputated parts of his body to appease his god Shiva.[2] This may sound shocking but it is simply the precursor of modern religions, which teach people to earn forgiveness through fasting or through pilgrimage or through good works or through charitable giving. The world's religions are all about *doing*, but the Western worldview arrogantly

1    *The Simpsons*, Season 10, Episode 15 – "Marge Simpson in: 'Screaming Yellow Honkers'" (1999).

2    Agamemnon and Ravana's sacrifices are recorded in Homer's *Iliad* and in the *The Ramayana*.

assumes that we don't have to do anything at all. Being a respectable Westerner is all it takes to win God's acceptance, so religion can be left to the uneducated masses of the developing world. Jesus cuts across this arrogance when he says he came to offer the true sacrifice for sin. The world's religions tell us what we need to *do*, but we always fail. Jesus tells us that he came so that we can rely on what he has *done* instead.

Jesus exposes the Western worldview as arrogant *because it assumes we can build our own path to reach God*. The American talk-show host Oprah Winfrey spoke for our culture as a whole when she shared her view that "*One of the biggest mistakes humans make is to believe there is only one way... There are many paths leading to what you call God.*"[3] That's the issue in a nutshell: People in our culture worship "*what you call God*". Jesus warns us that God made us in his image and that he won't allow us to return the favour. The true God is the true God, even if we try to redefine him. Man-made paths lead to man-made gods, but only one path leads to the true and living God. It is the path which God himself has prepared for us. It is the path which Jesus describes when he says, "*I am the Way.*"

Jesus exposes the Western worldview as arrogant *because it denies our need for God to send a Saviour*. Jesus' statement in John 14:6 is not an isolated one. He made it one of the major themes of his teaching that "*All who have come before me are thieves and robbers*" (John 10:8) and that "*Whoever believes in the Son has eternal life, but whoever rejects the Son will not see life, for God's*

---

3    Oprah made this comment on her talk show in 1998.

*wrath remains on them*" (John 3:36). When we consider that Jesus alone is fully God and fully man, it makes perfect sense that he should teach us that "*Whoever believes and is baptised will be saved, but whoever does not believe will be condemned*" (Mark 16:16). Since there is only one true Father and only true one Son, there can be only one true Saviour.

There is only one man who was born to a virgin in order to demonstrate that our hope for salvation does not depend on man's effort, but on a divine miracle. There is only one man in history who taught that our salvation relies not just on his teaching but on his identity.[4] Whereas Muhammad freely confessed that "*I am nothing new among the prophets; I do not know what will happen to me and to my followers; I am only a plain warner*" (Qur'an 46:9), Jesus taught very clearly that he *is* the Way, he *is* the Truth, he *is* the Life and he *is* the Resurrection. Others have claimed to speak words for God but only one man has had the authority to take the Old Testament Scriptures and declare, "*You have heard that it was said... **but I tell you**...*" (Matthew 5:21–48).

Jesus therefore exposes the Western worldview as arrogant *because it denies the uniqueness of Jesus and his cross*. It echoes Peter when he was rebuked by Jesus for attempting to persuade him that he did not truly need to die: "*Get behind me, Satan! You are a stumbling block to me; you do not have in mind the things of God, but the things of men*" (Matthew 16:23). It overlooks the fact that Jesus

---

4    For example, Muhammad admits in the Qur'an that he himself is a sinner and in need of a saviour (48:2).

prayed three times in the Garden of Gethsemane for the Father to save the world through something other than his impending crucifixion, then rose to his feet with a conviction that *"without the shedding of blood there is no forgiveness"* (Matthew 26:36–54 and Hebrews 9:22). It assumes that God was either too cruel to let Jesus know that his death was unnecessary or that Jesus was too dim-witted to hear God calling off the plan. It doesn't grasp how Jesus could promise a dying thief who had no time left for religious endeavours that *"Today you will be with me in Paradise"* (Luke 23:43) or how he declared all our religious efforts powerless to save us when he cried out triumphantly from the cross that *"It is done!"* (John 19:30). The Western worldview doesn't actually believe that all religions are equally valid. It believes that Christianity, the world's largest religion, is fundamentally wrong. Talk about arrogant.

We have journeyed long enough with the ungagged Jesus for each of us to be able to make a decision for ourselves. Will we conform to the lazy arrogance of our Western culture as it was expressed by John Lennon when he speculated that *"What Jesus and Mohammed and Buddha and all the rest said was right. It's just that the translations have gone wrong"*?[5] When John Lennon was assassinated in 1980, his ashes were scattered in New York's Central Park because everybody knew he was merely a human who had no power to overcome the grave. Will we listen instead to Muhammad, who died of a fever in the arms of one of his dozen wives, or to the Buddha who died of dysentery after eating

5    John Lennon said this in an interview in 1965.

an infected piece of pork? Muhammad was buried in Medina and the Buddha was cremated in India, because everybody knew that they were humans who had no power over the grave. Or will we listen to Jesus, who died and was buried and three days later rose from the grave in order to prove that he had just opened the only path to the real God? Will we be humble enough to surrender to Peter's conclusion after the resurrection that *"Salvation is found in no one else, for there is no other name under heaven given to mankind by which we must be saved"* (Acts 4:12)?

Let's shake off the arrogance of our Western worldview and embrace the true humility of Jesus' statement that he is the only way to God. Let's recognize that the different world religions are all about *doing* and that Jesus alone says it is *done*. Let's receive him as the God-given sacrifice for sin for people in every culture and nation.

Let's accept what the ungagged Jesus tells us: *"The work of God is this: to believe in the one he has sent"* (John 6:29).

# 13

# Jesus on Following Him

When people come to the point of deciding to follow Jesus, he doesn't stop offending them. He checks that they are ready by offending them more than ever. It may not sound very offensive to us, but that's largely because we don't understand what he is saying. He tells people who want to follow him that they need to be baptized.

Most of us find the notion of baptism entirely inoffensive. We tend to use it as a rite of passage for newborn babies, as a good excuse for a family gathering, or at best as an expression of our general hope that a baby will grow up to follow Jesus in the future. There is nothing particularly humiliating about a baby being sprinkled with water when its day-to-day life is already a long succession of baths and nappy changes. But our christening services have very little to do with what Jesus meant when he sent his disciples into all the world to preach the Gospel, commanding them to *"Go and make disciples of all nations, **baptising them** in the name of the Father and of the Son and of the Holy Spirit"* (Matthew 28:19). When Jesus told his would-be followers to be baptized, he was commanding them to die.

Jesus did not invent water baptism. The Jews created it to show Gentile converts that they were dirty. The Law of Moses had commanded God's People to wash anything which came into contact with faeces or fungus or menstrual blood or a dead body, so the Jewish rabbis told non-Jews that they needed to take a full body wash before they could be accepted as part of the People of God. They needed to confess that they were Gentile *"dogs"* and that even *"the daughters of Samaritans are as [dirty as] menstruating women from the cradle."*[1] If they wanted to recline on the Jewish couch, then they needed to take a bath like the dirty dogs they were.[2]

Jesus clashed with the Jewish rabbis over this issue of ceremonial washing, but his solution was not to do away with baptism altogether. He offended the Jews by commanding them to be baptized too, because the thing which stops us drawing near to God is not our race but our life of sin. John the Baptist preached this message, and it was probably one of the reasons why King Herod's Jewish wife persuaded her husband to

---

1    Jesus lampooned this racism with his tongue-in-cheek comment in Matthew 15:26. The quote about Samaritans comes from the Jewish Talmud (*Niddah* 4:1).

2    Mark 7:1–7 and Luke 11:38 use the Greek word *baptizō* to describe Jews washing their dirty hands and plates before dinner.

have him killed. Jesus endorsed John's teaching when he was himself baptized to demonstrate that "*It is proper for us to do this to fulfil all righteousness*" (Matthew 3:15). Very soon afterwards, Jesus "*was gaining and baptising more disciples than John*" (John 4:1). Jesus made baptism such a hallmark of his ministry that the apostles were in no doubt how to answer when people asked them what it meant to follow Jesus. They commanded the crowds to "*Repent and be baptised, every one of you, in the name of Jesus Christ for the forgiveness of your sins*" (Acts 2:38).

Jesus tells those who want to follow him to be baptized in water because it is an outward sign that we *admit* we are sinners who have no power to save ourselves. The prophet Elisha was unimpressed when the pagan general Naaman knocked on his door bearing gifts to ask for the Lord to heal him of his leprosy. He revealed the general's hard heart by refusing his gifts and commanding him to wash his body in the River Jordan. Naaman was furious and refused, but his skin was only cleansed when he humbled himself and proved his faith in God by doing what he said. Like Naaman, the apostle Paul struggled to accept the Gospel message that forgiveness is a gift which can't be earned, because he was a Pharisee obsessed with impressing God through his good deeds. He was only saved when a Christian challenged him three days after his Damascus Road vision: "*What are you waiting for? Get up, be baptised and wash your sins away, calling on his name*" (Acts 22:16). Jesus issues exactly the same challenge to anyone who wants to follow him today.

Jesus tells those who want to follow him to be baptized in water because it is an outward sign that we *believe* in the message of his death and resurrection. Whereas John's baptism was simply an admission that we are sinners, Paul explains that Christian baptism confesses something far greater (Acts 19:1–7). Jesus used the word baptism to refer to his death and resurrection (Mark 10:38–39) so it expresses our faith that, because Jesus died and rose again for us, we somehow died and rose again with him.[3] 1 Peter 3:20–21 likens Christian baptism to Noah's Flood, when the old world was swept away so that a new world could emerge from its watery tomb. Romans 6:3–5 agrees that "*All of us who were baptised into Christ Jesus were baptised into his death. We were therefore buried with him through baptism into death in order that, just as Christ was raised from the dead through the glory of the Father, we too may live a new life.*" If our faith does not propel us to the waters of baptism, it may not be faith in Jesus' death and resurrection at all.

Jesus tells those who want to follow him to be baptized in water because it is an outward sign that we *commit* our entire lives into God's hands. Dead people are free from the desires which gripped them during their lives, and people who are baptized confess that they are free from what enslaved them before their conversion. Paul tells us that "*You are all children of God through faith in Christ Jesus, for all of you who were*

---

3    See Romans 6:6–8; Galatians 2:20; Colossians 2:12, 20; 3:1, 3. This is why John 3:23 and Acts 8:36–39 suggest that people were buried under water rather than simply being sprinkled with water.

*baptised into Christ have clothed yourselves with Christ"* (Galatians 3:26–27). God doesn't turn caterpillars into butterflies by shouting at them that they should be flying, but by inviting them to step into a chrysalis. He doesn't turn new believers into Christians who reflect Christ by shouting commands at them either. He invites them into the waters of baptism so that they can emerge as new men and women on the other side. That's why in the gospels Jesus refused to let anyone follow him on their own terms. The whole caterpillar must enter the chrysalis. The whole person must die and be raised. We read:

> *As they were walking along the road, a man said to him, "I will follow you wherever you go." Jesus replied, "Foxes have dens and birds have nests, but the Son of Man has no place to lay his head." He said to another man, "Follow me." But he replied, "Lord, first let me go and bury my father." Jesus said to him, "Let the dead bury their own dead, but you go and proclaim the kingdom of God." Still another said, "I will follow you, Lord; but first let me go back and say goodbye to my family." Jesus replied, "No one who puts a hand to the plough and looks back is fit for service in the kingdom of God." (Luke 9:57–62)*

Baptism is very bad news for people who are unwilling to *admit*, *believe* and *commit*. I personally found Jesus' call to baptism very difficult because my parents had christened me as a child and were not pleased when I told them that their well-meaning act had not involved any faith on my part and bore little resemblance to

Jesus' command for me to identify with him in his death and resurrection. I struggled further because I had been confirmed as a teenager and saw it as a significant milestone in my faith. I needed to accept that neither water without faith nor faith without water constituted Christian baptism.

On the other hand, baptism is an amazing part of the Gospel message for anyone who is willing to *admit*, *believe* and *commit*. It tells us that God has raised us to new life in Jesus Christ and that, as we pass through the waters of baptism, we can leave our old lives behind. We live in a culture which is sick of watching Christians talk about Jesus but walk just like the world. Water baptism isn't simply a promise that we have died to our old life and been raised with Christ. It is a promise from God that he will enable us to live as new creations through his resurrection power.

Richard Wurmbrand was converted to Christ and baptized as a 29-year-old in Romania. Imprisoned by the Communists in a jail where it was every man for himself, he was determined to display the power of the Gospel to his fellow inmates. Looking back to the waters of his baptism, he asked for God's power to live each day as one who had died to his old life and been raised as a new creation to live like Jesus. He gave up his precious jacket to a hardened atheist named Josif and shared his meagre prison rations with him. Josif was so impressed that he asked Richard Wurmbrand to tell him about this Jesus whom he followed:

*Josif said, "We have read nearly everything Jesus said now, but still I wonder what He was like to know as a man." I said, "I'll tell you. When I was in Room Four there was a pastor who would give away everything he had – his last bit of bread, his medicine, the coat from his back. I have given these things also sometimes, when I wanted them for myself. But at other times when men were hungry and sick and in need I could be very quiet; I didn't care. This other pastor was really Christlike. You felt that just the touch of his hand could heal and calm. One day he talked to a small group of prisoners and one asked him the question you have asked me: 'What is Jesus like? I've never met anyone like the man you describe, so good and loving and truthful.' And the pastor replied, in a moment of great courage, simply and humbly, 'Jesus is like me.' And the man, who had often received kindness from the pastor, answered, smiling, 'If Christ was like you, then I love Him.' The times when one may say such a thing as that, Josif, are very rare. But to me that is what it means to be Christian. To believe in Him is not such a great thing. To become like Him is truly great." "Pastor, if Jesus is like you, then I love Him, too," Josif said.*[4]

Jesus tells us to *admit, believe* and *commit* to him if we want to follow him. Then he tells us to be baptized in water, and to emerge from the waters of baptism transformed and ready to live by his resurrection power.

---

4   Richard Wurmbrand in his book *In God's Underground* (1968).

# 14

# JESUS ON HOW MUCH HE NEEDS YOU

When I became a Christian, I actually thought I was doing God a favour. I thought Jesus was looking for gifted followers to help him build his Kingdom, and that he would be rather pleased that he had managed to enlist me. Looking back, I know that it sounds arrogant and pathetic, but I want to be honest with you about how I really felt. I have discovered since then that I was by no means alone. It seems that many of us have an overinflated view of how much Jesus really needs us.

I find it strangely encouraging that Jesus' twelve disciples fell into exactly the same error. Peter tried to negotiate a compensation package from Jesus in return for all that he had given up in order to become his disciple (Matthew 19:27). The mother of James and John tried to secure from Jesus the best seats in heaven for her two sons in return for the faithful service they had offered him on earth (Matthew 20:20–28). The disciples argued with one another over which of them Jesus needed the most (Luke 9:46), and continued to do so even at the Last Supper (Luke 22:24–30). Is it any wonder, then, that Jesus taught so much about the fact that he doesn't actually need any of us at all? If we want to follow the real Jesus then we mustn't try to gag him when he tells us that he is the one who does us a favour, not the other way around.

Jesus tells us that *we are not doing him a favour by accepting his offer of forgiveness*. When a rabbi flattered him that many of the Jewish rulers were willing to hail him as God's prophet, he didn't say thank you. He told the rabbi that the Jewish rulers needed to die and experience his resurrection life if they ever wanted to be saved (John 3:1–3). He made it clear that God isn't asking us to do him a favour by responding to the Gospel. He is asking us to die.[1]

On one of the occasions when he caught his disciples debating which one of them he needed most, Jesus deliberately offended them with his answer. He told them that *"the Son of Man did not come to be served, but to serve, and to give his life as a ransom for many"* (Mark 10:45). The Greek word for *ransom* in this verse is *lutron*, and it was a word which spoke of helplessness and pity. A man who was condemned to death for a capital crime was as good as dead unless somebody intervened to pay a *lutron* or *ransom price*

---

1   The rabbi, Nicodemus, responded to this challenge by separating himself from the Jewish ruling classes and sacrificing everything to identify with Jesus in his death and resurrection (John 7:50–52; 19:38–42).

to set him free. A soldier who was captured on the battlefield was destined to die as a prisoner of war unless somebody had mercy on him and paid a *lutron* or *ransom price* to bring him home. A common slave who was sold at the market knew that his only hope of freedom was for a rich person to take pity on him and pay a *lutron* or *ransom price* in order to set him free.[2] Jesus was therefore stating that we contribute nothing to our salvation except for our sin. This talk of slaves and criminals and prisoners of war was deeply insulting to the Romans, who dismissed people they disliked by accusing them of having *"the mind of a slave"*.[3] It was also deeply insulting to the Jews, who insisted furiously that *"We are Abraham's descendants and have never been slaves of anyone. How can you say that we shall be set free?"* (John 8:33).

Nevertheless, Jesus insisted that this is true. He doesn't want us to be fooled by smooth-talking preachers who flatter egos by telling us that God is like the famous British World War One poster, trying to recruit us into his army by promising that *"God needs you!"* The British army would not accept recruits during World War One unless they were healthy. Jesus makes it clear that God will not accept recruits into his army unless they admit that they are sick.

---

2    For non-biblical examples of this use of the word *lutron*, see Plato's *Laws* (11.4) and Josephus in *The Wars of the Jews* (2.14.1). For biblical examples, see Exodus 21:30, Leviticus 25:51–52 and Numbers 35:31–32 in the Greek Septuagint.

3    The Roman historian Tacitus says this as much about noblemen (*Histories*, 5.9) as he does about former slaves (*Annals*, 15.54).

Jesus also tells us that *we are not doing him a favour by becoming more like him in godly character*. He reserved his most stinging rebukes for religious people who patted themselves on the back for their advancement in Christian character, forgetting that each fresh breakthrough in godliness is simply a fresh experience of the Gospel which makes us even more indebted to God than before. We read in Luke 18:9–14 that

> *To some who were confident of their own righteousness and looked down on everyone else, Jesus told this parable: "Two men went up to the temple to pray, one a Pharisee and the other a tax collector. The Pharisee stood by himself and prayed: 'God, I thank you that I am not like other people – robbers, evildoers, adulterers – or even like this tax collector. I fast twice a week and give a tenth of all I get.' But the tax collector stood at a distance. He would not even look up to heaven, but beat his breast and said, 'God, have mercy on me, a sinner.' I tell you that this man, rather than the other, went home justified before God. For all those who exalt themselves will be humbled, and those who humble themselves will be exalted."*

Jesus warns us through this parable that religious people face a danger which irreligious people do not face. They are at risk of being more impressed by their own acts of obedience towards God than they are by Jesus' great act of obedience on the cross which set them free. Even our best acts of obedience to God are like filthy rags unless they are made acceptable through Jesus' death and resurrection (Isaiah 64:6; 1 Peter 2:5), and our best prayers and worship are only acceptable to God if they are purified through his blood (Revelation 8:3–5). Advancement in Christian character only comes through deeper experience of the Gospel. It doesn't make God more indebted to us. It makes us even more indebted to God.

John Calvin shook sixteenth-century Europe by preaching that the essence of salvation is admitting that we need God's help and that he does not need ours. He wrote that *"God cannot bear with seeing his glory appropriated by the creature in even the smallest degree, so intolerable to him is the sacrilegious arrogance of those who, by praising themselves, obscure his glory."*[4] He echoed the message of Luke 17:7–10, when Jesus warned:

*Suppose one of you has a servant ploughing or looking after the sheep. Will he say to the servant when he comes in from the field, "Come along now and sit down to eat"? Won't he rather say, "Prepare my supper, get yourself ready and wait on me while I eat and drink; after that you may eat and drink"? Will he thank the servant because he did what he was told to do? So you also, when you have done everything you were told to do, should say, "We are unworthy servants; we have only done our duty."*[5]

---

4    John Calvin says this while talking about Psalm 9:1 in his *Commentary on the Psalms* (1557).

5    Note the balance in Matthew 19:27–20:16. God will reward us for our faithful service to his Kingdom, but he will reward us based on his grace towards us and not on the basis of anything we have earned.

Jesus therefore warns us that *we are not doing him a favour by playing our part in his mission to the world*. He appeared to John, the last surviving disciple, in about 95 AD in order to give him the vision of God's work throughout history which we know as the book of Revelation. He gave John a vision of twenty-four elders in heaven, representing the twelve Jewish patriarchs and the twelve apostles, and he showed him how God's People ought to view their devoted service to God. John saw the twenty-four elders taking off their crowns of victory and throwing them down at Jesus' feet, proclaiming, *"You are worthy, our Lord and God, to receive glory and honour and power, for you created all things, and by your will they were created and have their being"* (Revelation 4:11). Every person we lead to Christ, every church we plant, and every breakthrough we achieve for the poor and needy in Jesus' name is the direct result of Jesus' power working through us. It hasn't made God indebted to us. It has made us even more indebted to God.

We have almost reached the end of this short book about the ungagged Jesus, so it is time for each of us to decide whether we will follow him. That's why it's so important that we grasp that we aren't doing him a favour by surrendering our lives to him. He isn't looking for strong helpers but for an army of weak people who see their lives for what they are and who gladly surrender them into the hands of their powerful Saviour. John Piper explains:

> *"The Son of Man… came not to be served"* (Mark 10:45). *The Bible is concerned to call us back*

*from idolatry to serve the true and living God (1 Thessalonians 1:9). But it is also concerned to keep us from serving the true God in the wrong way. There is a way to serve God that belittles and dishonours Him. Therefore, we must take heed... If Jesus said that He came not to be served, service may be rebellion...*

*God cannot be served in any way that implies we are meeting His needs... What is the greatness of our God? What is His uniqueness in the world?... All the other so-called gods make man work for them. Our God will not be put in the position of an employer who must depend on others to make his business go. Instead He magnifies His all-sufficiency by doing the work Himself. Man is the dependent partner in this affair. His job is to wait for the Lord.*

*What is God looking for in the world? Assistants? No. The gospel is not a help-wanted ad. It is a help-available ad. Nor is the call to Christian service a help-wanted ad. God is not looking for people to work for Him but people who let Him work mightily in and through them...*

*Any servant who tries to get off the divine dole and strike up a manly partnership with his Heavenly Master is in revolt against the Creator. God does not barter. He gives mercy to servants who will have it, and the wages of death to those who won't. Good service is always and fundamentally receiving mercy, not rendering assistance... The only right way to serve God is in a way that reserves for Him all the glory.*[6]

---

6    John Piper in *Brothers, We Are Not Professionals* (2003).

# 15

# JESUS ON DOING LIFE TOGETHER

We have reached the last of the fifteen most offensive sayings of Jesus. It is the last of the fifteen things which you are least likely to hear preached about in Western churches, and the last of the things which make most people want to gag him. If it feels like a bit of a let-down, the least controversial saying of Jesus in the whole book so far, then don't be fooled. That simply means you haven't grasped what it meant for Jesus and his twelve disciples to do life together. When we understand what it meant for Jesus to choose twelve disciples and to describe them as his new family, it's easy to see why many would-be followers of Jesus close their ears to the costly nature of this calling.

*Jesus went up on a mountainside and called to him those he wanted, and they came to him. He appointed twelve that they might be with him and that he might*

*send them out to preach and to have authority to*
*drive out demons. These are the twelve he appointed:*
*Simon (to whom he gave the name Peter), James son of*
*Zebedee and his brother John (to them he gave the name*
*Boanerges, which means "sons of thunder"), Andrew,*
*Philip, Bartholomew, Matthew, Thomas, James son*
*of Alphaeus, Thaddaeus, Simon the Zealot and Judas*
*Iscariot, who betrayed him.*

*Then Jesus entered a house, and again a crowd*
*gathered, so that he and his disciples were not even able*
*to eat. When his family heard about this, they went*
*to take charge of him, for they said, "He is out of his*
*mind."*

*Then Jesus' mother and brothers arrived. Standing*
*outside, they sent someone in to call him. A crowd was*
*sitting around him, and they told him, "Your mother*
*and brothers are outside looking for you."*

*"Who are my mother and my brothers?" he asked.*

*Then he looked at those seated in a circle around*
*him and said, "Here are my mother and my brothers!*
*Whoever does God's will is my brother and sister and*
*mother." (Mark 3:13–21, 31–35)*

When most people read this passage they major on how
wonderful it must have been for the Twelve to have
been called to be with Jesus. That's understandable
because it was an enormous privilege to be invited to
live for three years in close proximity to Jesus. What
must have been rather less attractive for the Twelve,
however, was living for three years in close proximity
to one another. There was a reason why we find them

fighting and arguing with one another throughout the gospels. Jesus had called a group of very different people to commit themselves to doing life together.

Take James and John, for example. They can't have been easy to live with. When Jesus nicknamed them *Boanerges*, he didn't mean it as a compliment. He called them the "sons of thunder" because they lost their temper very easily (Luke 9:51–56) and because they were shockingly self-assertive (Mark 10:35–41). Or take Simon the Zealot, who was part of a Jewish sect that expressed its zeal for God by refusing to pay any taxes to Caesar. It can't have been easy for him to spend three years with Matthew the former tax collector. Since Matthew had fleeced the tradesmen on the road out of Capernaum, where Peter and Andrew had their fishing business, it can't have been easy for them either. This is before we mention the regional prejudices between the lone southerner Judas and the eleven Galilean northerners, or the personality differences between Peter the loudmouthed optimist and Thomas the pessimistic doubter. Don't get so caught up in how great a privilege it was for the Twelve to be called to do life with Jesus that you miss how difficult it must have been for them to be called to do life with one another.

We live in a culture that despises organized religion, which is strange because we wouldn't send our children to a disorganized school or vote for a disorganized government. Our problem is not with organized religion at all, but with religion which refuses to let us follow God on our own terms. But that's precisely the reason why Jesus chose twelve disciples who were bound to clash with one another, because following him is not an individual affair. John Wesley was right when he taught that *"The Bible knows nothing of solitary religion."* Jesus deliberately created a church culture which is reflected in the New Testament commands to love *one another*, serve *one another*, teach *one another* and bear with *one another*.[1] We can't do life with Jesus unless we are willing to do life with one another.

Jesus insists that doing life together is *how we learn to be more like him*. Before I got married, I thought I was a very easy-going person. I only discovered how self-centred I was when I started sharing my life and home with another person. Before I was recruited into a highly competitive business environment, I thought I was a humble person. It was only when several of my new colleagues claimed credit for my work and started angling for promotion that I discovered just how self-assertive I could be. Before I became father to four children, I used to fool myself I was a very patient person. Doing life with other people always reveals to us the depth of sin which lurks hidden away in our hearts. That's why Jesus called the Twelve together for a season in order *"that he might send them out to preach"* the Gospel, because it is only in community that we learn to respond fully to the Gospel ourselves. How did Andrew feel when Jesus chose his three fishing partners Peter, James and John to form his inner circle

---

1    In his letter to the Romans alone, Paul refers to *"one another"* in 1:12, 12:5, 12:10, 12:16, 13:8, 14:13, 14:19, 15:5, 15:7, 15:14 and 16:16.

of three disciples but decided not to choose him? How did Matthew feel when Jesus overlooked his financial experience and chose Judas to manage the disciples' money instead (John 12:4–6)? Doing life together can be painful but it is also very fruitful.

We need to recognize that we live in a highly individualistic culture, which is actively opposed to the kind of community which Jesus is building. That is the reason why Christian commitment to gathering for Sunday services is at an all-time low, and why commitment to midweek fellowship groups is even lower still. We miss the point when we argue that we are busy, that we have enough friends already or that we don't want to be part of a formal church small group. The friends we choose to do life with tend to be of a similar age and race and education to ourselves, so they cannot challenge our sinful hearts in the same way as the diverse mishmash of people Jesus assembles together as his Church. The Bible tells us that *"The heart is deceitful above all things and beyond cure. Who can understand it?"* (Jeremiah 17:9), and Jesus tells us that sharing life with a diverse group of Christians is part of the solution. He warns us not to despise any of those he has saved (Matthew 18:10) because each believer can point out our sin (Matthew 18:15–17), can help our prayers to be heard in heaven (Matthew 18:19) and can help us to experience more of God's presence (Matthew 18:20). No wonder 1 Peter 2:17 warns us that the mark of a healthy Christian is that they *"love the family of believers"*.

Jesus also insists that doing life together is *how we wrench our selfish eyes away from ourselves and onto serving others*. I have never met a Christian who didn't want to pour out their life for Jesus in the abstract, but what really matters is our willingness to pour out our lives for Jesus in the concrete reality of church life. When Peter told Jesus three times that he loved him in John 21:15–17, Jesus replied each time with a concrete command to *"Feed my lambs"*, *"Take care of my sheep"* and *"Feed my sheep"*. Peter obeyed him on the Day of Pentecost by organizing those who followed Jesus into large-scale meetings in the Temple courtyards and into smaller fellowship groups who broke bread together in each other's homes (Acts 2:42–47). Peter encouraged anyone who wanted to follow Jesus to be *"added to their number"*, and he was so adamant that this was part and parcel of the Christian life that his converts *"devoted themselves to the apostles' teaching and to fellowship… All the believers were together and had everything in common."*

Jesus also insists that doing life together is *how we add our weight to the advance of the Gospel*. Most of the reasons we give for neglecting fellowship with other Christians revolve around ourselves – it's too inconvenient or too time-consuming or too painful – but Jesus tells us that this is the price his followers have to pay in order to carry his Gospel deep into the heart of every nation. It is very telling that when Jesus told his followers to go and make disciples they responded by planting churches. It is also very telling that they copied the pattern of church meetings and structured fellowship which they had pioneered in Jerusalem after the Day of Pentecost. Do you want to push back Satan's rule in the world? Then Jesus promises you in Matthew 16:18 that *"I will build my church, and the gates of hell will not overcome it."* Do you want to display the glory of the invisible God to the unreached nations of the world? Then 1 John 4:12 tells you that *"No one has ever seen God, but if we love one another, God lives in us"*. The Devil is desperate to gag Jesus on this issue and to make us try to live out our Christian lives in splendid isolation from one another. He is currently succeeding in the Western world. If we want to follow Jesus then we mustn't let him.

So as we draw to the end of Jesus' fifteen most offensive teachings, don't gloss over the importance of Jesus' insistence that following him means doing life together. Don't miss the fact that the Christian faith conquered the Roman Empire because believers *"gave themselves first of all to the Lord, and then by the will of God also to us"* (2 Corinthians 8:5). Don't be fooled by our consumer culture into thinking you can construct a Christian experience of your own through sermon downloads, Christian TV and worship experiences courtesy of iTunes.

Because Jesus isn't coming back for individuals but for a Bride, for a City, for a People, for a Body and for a fellowship of believers who do life together. If you can't find a perfect church in your area, then find an imperfect one and make it better. Find a place where you can become more like Jesus, where you can serve other people and where you can add your weight to the advance of the Gospel. Find a church where you can look around and say with Jesus: *"Here are my mother and my brothers! Whoever does God's will is my brother and sister and mother."*

# CONCLUSION:
# GAGGING JESUS

Peter had been listening to Jesus for two years. It was time for Jesus to ask him a question: *"Who do people say I am?"*

We started this book by answering that question. We saw that Communists claim Jesus was a Communist, capitalists claim he was a capitalist, dictators claim he was a dictator, civil rights campaigners claim he was a civil rights campaigner and respectable Westerners claim he was as refined and respectable as they are. Everybody wants to claim Jesus as their friend, but it's suspicious that the Jesus they have befriended looks so very similar to themselves. They are following a gagged-and-bound Jesus, a Jesus of their own making, a ventriloquist's dummy that they can sit on their knee and make say the things they want to hear.

After Peter had answered this first question, Jesus asked him another one. He asked him: *"What about you? Who do you say I am?"* You can read about their conversation in Matthew 16, but Jesus doesn't want you to dodge this question by pretending that he is asking it of somebody other than you. We have reached the final chapter of *Gagging Jesus*, and Jesus turns to you and asks you to make a decision. You have been watching and listening to him for long enough. Who do you say that he really is?

Will you be like the American president Thomas Jefferson, who got offended and tried to gag Jesus? He insisted he was a Christian,[1] but he literally took a razorblade to the gospels and chopped out the words he didn't want to hear. He constructed his own *Jefferson Bible* in 1820, which contains none of Jesus' miracles, none of his claims to be God and nothing about his resurrection. In the same year that he produced this gagged-and-bound Jesus, he boasted to one of his friends that *"We are not afraid to follow truth wherever it may lead."*[2] Will you protest your open-mindedness like Thomas Jefferson, while gagging Jesus whenever his words offend you?

Or will you be like Napoleon Bonaparte, who boasted that he respected the real Jesus but who made very little personal response to what Jesus actually said? Shortly before he died in exile, he confessed to one of his closest friends that,

*I know men, and I tell you that Jesus Christ is not a man… Jesus came into the world to reveal the mysteries of heaven and the laws of the Spirit. Alexander, Caesar, Charlemagne, and myself have*

1    He insisted on this point very strongly in a letter to Benjamin Rush on 21st April 1803.
2    He wrote this in a letter to William Roscoe on 27th December 1820.

*founded empires. But upon what did we rest the
creations of our genius? Upon force! Jesus Christ alone
founded his empire upon love, and at this moment
millions of men would die for him. I die before my time,
and my body will be given back to earth, to become food
for worms. Such is the fate of him who has been called
the great Napoleon. What an abyss between my deep
misery and the eternal kingdom of Christ, which is
proclaimed, loved, and adored, and which is extended
over the whole earth! Call you this dying? Is it not
living, rather?"*[3]

Napoleon understood that Jesus is God, but he shrank
back from surrendering his life to him. He had once
boasted that *"By turning Catholic I ended the war in
the Vendée, by becoming a Moslem I established myself in
Egypt, by becoming an ultramontane I won the Italians. If I
were governing a country of Jews, I would rebuild the temple
of Solomon."*[4] He had become so used to gagging Jesus
and to using religion as a tool in his lust for power that
he died without ever responding to the real Jesus, for
all he claimed to admire him.

Or will you respond like some of the people we
have encountered during the course of this book,
who discovered the real Jesus and let their discovery
change their lives completely? Will you surrender
your possessions to him like Francis of Assisi? Will you

---

3    Napoleon said this to General Montholon, quoted by John
Abbott in *The Life of Napoleon Bonaparte* (1860).
4    He said this to Comte Pierre Louis Roederer in August 1800.
Quoted by Alexander Grab in *Napoleon and the Transformation of
Europe* (2003).

surrender fame and fortune like Charles T. Studd? Will you serve him courageously like Dietrich Bonhoeffer and Desmond Tutu? Will you surrender your family to him like my friend Hannah when she turned her back on Islam, or your sexual preferences like my friend Paul when he turned his back on his gay lifestyle? Will you say no to worry and to bitterness and to pornography? Will you accept him as the Son of God and as the only Saviour of the world? Will you die to your old life like Richard Wurmbrand and let him preach his Gospel to the world through your resurrection lifestyle?

Jesus waited for Peter to answer him. Finally, Peter made his decision: *"You are the Messiah, the Son of the Living God."*

Jesus responded: *"Blessed are you, Simon son of Jonah, for this was not revealed to you by flesh and blood, but by my Father in heaven."* (Matthew 16:16–17)

God the Father has also been speaking to you through this short book. Jesus is waiting for your reply. If you started reading this book as a non-Christian, he is waiting to see if you will admit your sin, believe in his sacrifice and commit the rest of your life to following him. If you started reading this book as a Christian, he is waiting to see if you will follow the pocket-sized Jesus who is found in many churches – who dances to our tune, plays by our rules and says whatever we want to hear – or whether you will follow the ungagged Jesus as we have discovered him in all his offensive glory. If you will, then you will discover that convincing people that the Gospel message is true isn't actually very difficult. We simply have to believe it wholeheartedly ourselves and to start living as if it is really true.

So don't put this book down without answering Jesus' question: *"Who do you say I am?"*

Jesus stands before you in his ungagged glory. He asks you to surrender the rest of your life to him and to start following him with all your heart today.

# Next Steps: Walking Daily with the Ungagged Jesus

Surrendering your life to Jesus isn't the end of the story. It is only the beginning. It is the start of an exciting journey with the ungagged Jesus, and I would like to help you with the next steps on your journey.

## Online Sermons

This book was based on a series of sermons that I preached with my friend David Featherstone at Everyday Church, the church we lead together in Southwest London.

We make our sermons available online free of charge, both as videos and as audio files, in order to help people to follow the real Jesus. If you think that this might help you in your next steps with the ungagged Jesus, then you can find all of our latest sermons at **www.everyday.org.uk/sermons**.

## Blog and Twitter

I also try to help people to follow the ungagged Jesus through my blog and through my daily messages on Twitter. You can find my blog at **www. philmoorelondon.com** and you can follow me on Twitter by searching for **@philmoorelondon.**

## Reading the Bible

I truly believe that the biggest help I can give you, however, is to help you to read and understand the Bible. That's why I have written a series of devotional commentaries in a similar style to *Gagging Jesus*. They will take you through each of the books of the Bible, explaining what each passage says, challenging you to face up to what that means and then helping you to apply it to your life. You can find all of the books in the *Straight to the Heart* series of commentaries on Amazon, at any good book retailer or by visiting **www.philmoorebooks.com.**

Jesus is calling you to set out on a lifetime of walking with him. My prayer is that these resources will help you to follow the ungagged Jesus every day.

# **STRAIGHT TO THE HEART** SERIES:

## OLD TESTAMENT

ISBN 978 0 85721 001 2

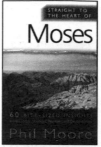

ISBN 978 0 85721 056 2

ISBN 978 0 85721 252 8

ISBN 978 0 85721 428 7

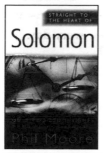

ISBN 978 0 85721 426 3

## NEW TESTAMENT

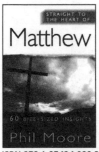

ISBN 978 1 85424 988 3

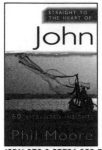

ISBN 978 0 85721 253 5

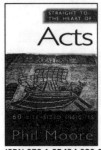

ISBN 978 1 85424 989 0

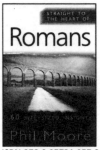

ISBN 978 0 85721 057 9

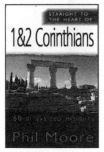

ISBN 978 0 85721 002 9

ISBN 978 1 85424 990 6